in Britain

KT-437-555

WITHDRAWN

Books in the Politics Study Guides series

Democracy
in Britain

Matt Cole

Edinburgh University Press

To Sue and Jessie

© Matt Cole, 2006

Edinburgh University Press Ltd
22 George Square, Edinburgh

Typeset in 11/13pt Monotype Baskerville by
Servis Filmsetting Ltd, Manchester, and
printed and bound in Great Britain by
Antony Rowe Ltd, Chippenham, Wilts

A CIP record for this book is available from the British Library

ISBN-10 0 7486 2312 4 (paperback)
ISBN-13 978 0 7486 2312 9 (paperback)

The right of Matt Cole to be identified as author of this work has been
asserted in accordance with the Copyright, Designs and Patents Act 1988.

Published with the support of the Edinburgh University Scholarly
Publishing Initiatives Fund.

Contents

Part II: Practice

Boxes

'Democracy is acknowledged folly.'

> Alcibiades, Athenian statesman and soldier (450–404 BC)

'Where the poor rule, it is democracy.'

> Aristotle, Greek philosopher (384–322 BC)

'As soon as public service ceases to be the main concern of the citizens and they prefer to serve that state with their purse rather than their person, the state is already close to ruin. Thanks to laziness and money, they end up with soldiers to enslave their country and deputies to sell it.'

> Jean-Jacques Rousseau, Genevan philosopher (1712–82)

'When I refuse to obey an unjust law, I do not contest the right of the majority to command, but I simply appeal from the sovereignty of the people to the sovereignty of mankind. Some have not feared to assert that a people can never out step the boundaries of justice and reason. But that is the language of a slave.'

> Alexis de Tocqueville, French aristocrat (1805–59)

'The idea of rational democracy is not that the people themselves govern, but that they have security for good government . . . The best government must be the government of the wisest, and these must always be few.'

> John Stuart Mill, radical liberal philosopher and MP (1806–73)

'Alongside an immense expansion of democracy, which for the first time becomes democracy for the poor, democracy for the people, and not for the moneybags, the dictatorship of the proletariat brings about a series of restrictions on the freedom of the oppressors.'

> V. I. Lenin, Russian revolutionary leader (1870–1924)

'The democratic method is the institutional arrangement for arriving at political decisions in which individuals acquire the power to decide by means of a competitive struggle for the people's vote.'

> Joseph Schumpeter, Austrian-American economist (1883–1950)

'Democracy without order is impossible. The political parties are not fit to assume the onerous responsibility of running this proud nation. We will create a new democracy, with the army continuing as our great protectors.'

> General Augusto Pinochet, Chilean military dictator (1915–)

'Democracy is hypocrisy. If democracy means freedom, why aren't our people free? If democracy means justice, why don't we have justice? If democracy means equality, why don't we have equality?'

Malcolm X, US black nationalist leader (1925–65)

'After 18 years of one-party rule, people want change, believe that it is necessary for the country and for democracy, but require faith to make the change. The Conservatives seem opposed to the very idea of democracy. There is unquestionably a national crisis of confidence in our political system, to which Labour will respond in a measured and sensible way.'

Britain Deserves Better, Labour Manifesto, 1997

'Here you have a Labour government that is clearly going to be returned on the basis of something like 42% of the popular vote – a share of the popular vote, incidentally, that would have led to an opposition party being massacred a generation ago. It looks, on the basis of this tiny turnout, as though only one in four eligible voters in the entire country will have voted Labour – and yet it has this huge majority and of course will claim a mandate to govern.

Professor Anthony King, on the night of the 2001 General Election

'The United Kingdom has just completed its periodic exercise in representational democracy. The result – the re-election of a Labour government with a severely depleted majority – was probably a reasonable reflection of the people's will. How far it was either representational or democratic is another matter. Thoroughgoing reform of the electoral system needs to be embarked upon now, before faith in the system is lost entirely.'

'A Strategy to Revive an Outdated Democracy', *The Independent*, 10 May 2005

'Democracy isn't just a Western idea. It's what people, wherever they're given the chance to have it, want.

Tony Blair, *Sunday AM*, BBC1, 25 September 2005

Introduction

Properly understood, the discipline of politics is always about power, and democracy is one basis for distributing power. The character of power, its location, its uses and the justifications of its uses – these central issues are always part of the subject matter concerning students of politics. It is the claim of democracy, or at least of some of its adherents, to have found the most moral way of exercising power, and it is usually the boast of British governments that theirs is the country in which this has been most successfully achieved. The evidence supporting and questioning these two claims is the focus of this book.

Britain has claimed to be a democracy for well over a century. After the Third Reform Act enfranchised most men in 1884, A. V. Dicey acknowledged that, despite the doctrine of parliamentary sovereignty to which he was attached, 'the electors in the long run always enforce their will';[1] Dicey went on to consider the relationship between public opinion and the law, and even anticipated the use of referendums in Britain. The year 1918 was regarded by many as the true birth date of British democracy because, after it, only women under thirty were excluded from the franchise – and this was rectified ten years later. Clement Attlee, whose post-war government ended plural voting and curtailed the powers of the House of Lords, expressed his pride in 'Britain, the home of the most successful democracy on a large scale'.[2] Prime Ministers from Harold Wilson to Margaret Thatcher and Tony Blair have all expressed the same pride and confidence. But each of these claims, even if sincere, understands democracy in a different way – and so have all similar claims in other times and places. Despite growing misgivings, there remains a widespread presumption in British politics that democracy is best, and that Britain is democratic. Neither of these is beyond question and, indeed, the latter has been especially widely questioned in recent years. The purpose of this book is to examine critically both of these presumptions.

It is ironic that the principles of democracy, to which nearly all in politics declare loyalty at the beginning of the twenty-first century, have been neglected for most of the period since their first development over 2,500 years ago. In his celebrated work on 'the end of history', American theorist Francis Fukuyama claimed in 1989 that liberal democracy had seen off all competing political systems, but Fukuyama has been forced more recently to modify that boast in the face of the global strength of various theocratic or other non-democratic movements;[3] certainly most regimes and movements in most parts of the world for most of history since the invention of democracy would not have recognised the term; most of those that did would have regarded it with suspicion or hostility.

Today, democracy must be the most overworked and debased concept in politics. It is, as Professor Bernard Crick remarked, 'perhaps the most promiscuous word in the world of public affairs. She is everybody's mistress and yet somehow retains her magic even when a lover sees her favours being illicitly shared by another' (an analogy which might itself earn the indignation of feminists for being undemocratic in its treatment of women).[4] Few writers and politicians will condemn democracy (although, as we shall see, few are committed to it as a first principle either); few countries declare themselves to be anything less than democratic in their aspirations at least, if not their practice. Democracy is the badge worn by leading political parties of the Left in America, the Right in Japan, the extreme Right in Russia and the opposition in Zimbabwe. In Britain it is claimed by the Liberal Democrats, the Democratic Unionist Party and the former Communists who went on to be known as the Democratic Left. Stalinist satellite states, revolutionary China, Latin-American military regimes, all are as proud of their democratic heritage as have been Aristotle, J. S. Mill, Lenin, Churchill, Castro and General Pinochet. We hear of Tory Democracy, Liberal Democracy, Democratic Centralism and even Totalitarian Democracy: to ask the real democrats to step forward from this array of suitors to the title is bold indeed. More than bold, it is folly.

It is this universality of the claim to democracy, and particularly its central place in the British political self-image, that makes it both complex and vital. Few political conversations in the twenty-first century can be understood without a grasp of the meaning of the term, and yet its meaning is evidently an unfixed and fiercely disputed matter. Part I of this book explores the different meanings which have been attributed to democracy, and the way in which it relates to the principal traditions of political theory. What will emerge from this is that each of the versions of democracy which has developed has considerable weaknesses, and fits imperfectly even with the other ideas of those who promote it. In Part II, the British political system will be tested against the values of democracy it claims to reflect, and recent criticisms of the system, and recent attempts to improve it, will be evaluated. Part I is therefore predominantly theoretical in character; Part II is directly concerned with practical events, but all elements of the material tackled here involve evaluation – whether of ideas or of institutions. All of these questions are matters of fundamental argument and of profound importance to politics in modern Britain. The evidence examined in what follows is drawn mostly from the turn of the twenty-first century, partly from the pattern of modern history, and it also visits classical times; but it throws light upon discussions about any field of British politics today and for the foreseeable future.

PART I: THEORY

CHAPTER 1

Representation, Liberty and Democracy

Contents

Overview

Before examining the idea of democracy, it is useful to establish its relationship with two other commonplace concepts in modern political vocabulary, representation and liberty. Each has numerous varied interpretations, and these are reflected in modern day-to-day-politics. This chapter examines these different conceptions, their historical origins and examples of how they might be used in modern politics. It also examines arguments about their relevance and priority as political tools, and how these arguments are treated in the main traditions of British political thought: conservatism, liberalism and socialism. After reading this chapter, you should be able to distinguish between these versions of the ideas, and come to your own evaluation of them.

Key issues to be covered in this chapter

- How do the concepts of representation, democracy and liberty differ from one another in principle?
- How are these differences reflected in the practical reality of politics?
- Why is each of these ideas closely linked with democracy?
- How is each concept treated by the main political traditions in Britain?
- What different interpretations of each of the terms are used, and which stands greatest scrutiny?
- How do we resolve conflicts between these three concepts?

Interpretations of the terms

Representation, liberty and democracy are commonly, but wrongly, regarded as interchangeable terms. While in modern British politics each is usually presumed to entail the other, each can exist, and some have said can only exist, without the other. A barrister may represent a client, or a monarch a kingdom, without one being instructed, or even chosen, by the other; the House of Commons may be elected democratically, yet it may be markedly unrepresentative of the social characteristics, the interests and often the opinions of those who voted for it. Indeed, although MPs are elected, they are bound in constitutional theory to represent those in their constituencies who did not or could not vote for them. As for liberty, the traditional rights of the English to a fair trial, freedom of thought, faith and speech were hailed long before Britain was ever described as a democracy. On the other hand, the governments of democracies, including Britain, are regularly accused today by **civil liberties** groups of curtailing or negating these freedoms, sometimes because the public demands it: this dilemma has been a particular problem for recent Home Secretaries in determining the sentences available for those convicted of killing or abusing children, or the issue of whether to confirm or relax those sentences in individual cases such as the killers of Jamie Bulger. As these examples indicate, each of these terms also has a wide variety of interpretations by which it may be understood, and which imply quite contrary propositions in different contexts.

Representation

The term 'representation' entered English from Latin and Old French, and literally refers to the bringing into existence of something previously not present in a particular place or form. Originally, this usually meant the representation of an intangible quality or force, such as religious faith, or physical courage, which might be represented by a statue or painting. Only later, particularly following the Renaissance, was it considered possible to represent people or their particular ideas in political institutions such as church councils or parliaments. Some writers have argued that modem theories of representation date back to the church schism of 1378 over the procedure for choosing the

Pope; a more evolutionary and even unintentional development can be identified in the role of the English Parliament from its origins in 1215 (when membership of it was considered a tiresome monarchical imposition) to the time of Henry VIII and particularly in the controversies of the Civil War and Glorious Revolution of the seventeenth century. The presumption slowly arose that groups of men, or the institutions of which they were members, could be said to act on behalf of other, larger groups. Using eighteenth-century liberal theory, it was argued by American revolutionaries that there should be 'no taxation without representation', and in the French Revolution that 'all citizens have the right, personally or through their representatives, to have demonstrated to them the necessity of public taxes'. Thus, representation had moved from being a means of conveying appeals to those with divine authority, to being a conduit for the popular consent that legitimated government itself in liberal thought. Only in the nineteenth and the early twentieth centuries did the idea gain ground that a person could not represent others without being personally and secretly chosen by them in competition with others – the idea that democracy and representation are necessarily linked.

Throughout this process, the concept of representation has possessed several meanings – most of them concurrently. Key studies of representation – notably Hannah Pitkin's *The Concept of Representation*[1] – identify four principles or types, all of which are essential to political debate today, and all of which apply to modern politicians at one time or another.

Types of representation

1 Symbolic The simplest and least political (in the sense of denoting a claim to authority) sort of representation is that which merely involves 'standing for', as a flag represents a nation, a mark on a map a place, and a piece represents a player in a board game. The representation involved is no more than physical – a tangible presence denoting the intended presence of another person or persons. It is in this sense alone that a modern constitutional monarch such as the Queen represents the nation and perhaps its feelings, and government ministers may equally represent the Crown, or the public, on ceremonial occasions such as overseas state funerals or celebrations.

In the same way, even directly elected politicians, such as MPs, perform purely symbolic representative functions, such as presentations of awards to local schools or businesses.

2 Social Representativeness is meant by opinion pollsters, for example, to indicate the quality of reflecting the significant social characteristics of a wider group. A representative sample, therefore, is one which has the same proportions of men and women, rich and poor, urban and rural, black and white, or young and old, as the population at large, an impression of whose opinion is being sought. Parliament is in this sense a very unrepresentative institution, with far more middle-aged, middle-class, white men than there are among the electorate. Even the 2005 House of Commons, which has an historically unprecedented number of women and ethnic minority MPs, is a distorted mirror of British society (see Box 1.1). This has been the source of much criticism of the Commons in recent years, and all main parties have made specific efforts to encourage greater numbers of successful parliamentary candidates who are women or from ethnic minorities. The Labour Party, in particular, adopted a policy of drawing up women-only shortlists for the nomination of half of their candidates in Labour-held or winnable constituencies after 1993. This practice survived less than three years before being ruled illegal in an industrial tribunal in January 1996 but, by this stage, thirty-eight candidates had been chosen from women-only shortlists, and the following general election saw the largest ever number of women MPs – particularly Labour women MPs – by some distance. A modified version of the practice continues, and the Fawcett Society supports it as 'the reason Labour is so far ahead of the other two main parties'. Pressure to nominate more black and Asian candidates has been applied in all main parties since the 1980s, first by the Labour Party Black Sections movement, and latterly by Operation Black Vote, and it was in 1987 that the first ethnic minority MPs of modern times were returned. All three main parties have since then succeeded in securing the election of at least one ethnic minority MP. The total in 1987 – four – had risen to only fifteen by 2005, however, whereas a socially representative Commons would include over fifty MPs from ethnic minorities.

Pressure has also been applied to improve the proportion of women and ethnic minorities among appointments to public bodies,

Box 1.1 Social composition of the House of Commons, May 2005 onwards

House of Commons, 2005	Actual number of MPs	Representative number of MPs
Women	128	336
Ethnic minorities	15	51
University education	440	206
Oxbridge education	164	4
Private school	206	45
Age under 30	3	106
Age over 65	43	135
Professional	242	72
Manual worker	38	239

Some people seem to be better represented than others: How does this come about? And does it matter?

such as QUANGOs, and in senior civil service posts. This was reflected in John Major's 'Opportunity 2000' initiative of 1991, which committed fourteen major public- and private-sector employers to targets for the appointment of more women by the end of the century; it was also recognised in June 2005 by government minister Jim Murphy in response to a question in the Commons from Keith Vaz, the first Asian MP of modern times. Vaz complained that 'the number of women and ethnic minority people who serve on QUANGOs, is still woefully inadequate'; Murphy promised 'a series of new initiatives aims to ensure that bodies that serve the public more accurately represent society as a whole'. These bodies, being appointed rather than elected, are, of course, in no sense democratic; but they are seeking to be socially representative.

Indeed, this approach has led to counter-criticism from those who believe that such 'social engineering' or 'rigging' of parliamentary elections is undemocratic because it limits the free choice of representatives by electors, thus making Parliament less representative in terms of interpretations 3 and 4 (see below). This objection gave rise to the election in 2005 of Peter Law in Blaenau Gwent where, as a local Labour activist, Law had been prevented from seeking the Party's nomination by a decision from headquarters to use a women-only shortlist. Ironically, this debate serves only to illustrate the breadth of common ground on this subject, because **social representation** is rarely sought – even by the advocates of positive discrimination – *per se*. The desire for greater social representativeness in a body – whether an opinion-poll sample, a party conference or a parliament – is usually driven by the presumption that it is a precondition of representing the wider population's interests or opinions. Is it just, for example, that most race-relations legislation in Britain was passed by an all-white House of Commons; that women's rights to abortion were determined by a Commons that had fewer than one female MP in ten, or that Anti-Social Behaviour Orders aimed at controlling young people, and rising university tuition fees, were introduced by a Commons in which scarcely a single member was under thirty, and few came from a home with an income below the national average? The answer we give to this question must have reference to the consequences of social representation as well as to that representation in itself. Thus, although this interpretation of the representation is a distinct one, it is secondary, or at any rate not independent.

3 Interest The traditional meaning of 'representation' in British constitutional convention refers to the acts of protecting and promoting a person's or group's interests – that is, securing their well-being, usually entailing their long-term aims. This is the sense in which barristers represent their clients, and the role in which eighteenth-century philosopher Edmund Burke famously saw British MPs in his 'Speech to the electors of Bristol' (1774) in which he argued that 'your representative owes you, not his industry only, but his judgement; and he betrays instead of serving you, if he sacrifices it to your opinion' (see Box 1.2). This interpretation of representation presumes a large element of independence on the part of the representative, for the interests of the people he or she represents (as perceived by the representative) may not coincide with the opinion of those people as to their own interests. This is often reflected in differences of opinion on law-and-order issues: a classic example is the issue of capital punishment, the reintroduction of which has repeatedly been rejected by the Commons, despite some MPs' open acknowledgement that this contradicts the wishes of the clear majority of the general public they

Box 1.2 The MP as representative

Source A: From Edmund Burke's 'Letter to the Electors of Bristol',
1774
'Certainly, gentlemen, it ought to be the happiness and glory of a representative to live in the strictest union, the closest correspondence
and the most unreserved communication with his constituents. Their
wishes ought to have great weight with him; their opinions high
respect; their business unremitted attention. It is his duty to sacrifice
his repose, his pleasure, his satisfactions, to theirs; and above all,
ever, and in all cases, to prefer their interest to his own. But his unbi-
ased opinion, his mature judgement, his enlightened conscience, he
ought not to sacrifice to you, to any man, or to any set of men living.'

Source B: From George Gardiner MP, writing in the Sunday Express,
15 May 1988
'Very soon now MPs will be called on to vote yet again on the issue
that never goes away – should capital punishment be restored to our
judicial system? When the moment comes I will vote for the death
penalty, as I have always done, in whatever form the question is put
and for the same fundamental reason . . . I know there is at least a
3–1 chance that you, the reader, will agree with me . . . The majority
of MPs will vote against us, just like last time. It doesn't matter what
we think. And this, to be honest, is what will probably happen . . . We
shall be told that this is a moral issue, on which each MP must vote
according to his conscience. Edmund Burke will be wheeled out
again, arguing that MPs must exercise their own judgement and not
act as delegates . . . The public's view has never been in doubt.
Indeed, all the opinion poll evidence – going back before abolition in
1965 – is remarkably consistent . . . Now the latest count, after 23
years' experience of abolition, shows 73% of the public still telling
MPs that we have got it wrong . . . So what kind of "conscience" is
it that permits MPs to go on blocking the consistently expressed will
of the people over so many years? What kind of "moral right" justifies them in elevating their own opinion – honestly held, no doubt –
above the clear opinion of those who have elected them?'

Source C: from Blair's Hundred Days, *Derek Draper (Faber & Faber*
1997). Draper, who was Peter Mandelson's assistant, is describing
the first meeting of the Parliamentary Labour Party after the 1997
election.
'Tony Blair strides in from the right and cheers the new Members to
their feet. All but Dennis Skinner give him a standing ovation in return.

Blair rams home his message to any malcontents. "It was", he beams, "New Labour wot won it." The Parliamentary Labour Party, he says, was not elected to obstruct the government's mandate. It was elected to implement the manifesto, the early version of which was supported in a ballot by 95% of Labour Party members. The PLP, the government, and the Labour Party's activists and members are to act as one. The head cannot be separated from the body, and so the Party and the government must work in unison to achieve what they have both signed up to. "By all means, speak your mind", Blair concludes, "but remember what you were sent here to do." '

Source D: from Tess Kingham, writing in The Independent on Sunday, *10 June 2001*
'MPs who were elected for the first time last week will be excitedly awaiting their arrival in the Commons, and keen to make their mark. They are in for a shock. They are likely to become as disillusioned with our parliamentary system as the voters who stayed away from the polls – and, indeed, as I have become after four years in Parliament . . . Obviously I expected collective responsibility, but not for this to be ruthlessly enforced when there has been no collective decision-making. The new MPs will be bemused that they are expected to unquestioningly support controversial legislation that was never in the party manifesto, or discussed at any of the party's policy-making forums . . . For MPs who question or oppose – even once, and even if on behalf of constituents – the whipping system can be ruthless. At first I was in favour with the whips. When I challenged their authority and refused to vote for cuts to single-parent benefits or disability benefits (I could not square with my conscience the harm it would do to my constituents, and it was not part of our manifesto) the attitude changed. My constituency was threatened with the withdrawal of resources by one whip. Another told me that if I continued to be "awkward", my political career was finished . . . The control and manipulation of our elected representatives is [sic] an affront to democracy.'

Source E: Bill Morris, General Secretary, Transport and General Workers' Union, in the Foreword to Our House? Race and Representation in British Politics, *Rushanara Ali and Colm O'Cinneide (2002)*
'I am concerned about the detrimental impact that the continuing absence of non-white faces in front-line politics is having on the health of our democracy. If ethnic minorities cannot identify with the politicians who represent them, then they will have little reason to feel enthused about engaging in the political process. In the light of

recent events – including the riots of the summer of 2001 and the growing unease among British Muslims since September 11th – it is more important than ever before that we act to ensure that our political institutions provide the space for different sections of the community to participate in the mainstream political process. Unfair representation leads to political alienation, electoral disengagement and the erosion of democratic legitimacy.'

What views are offered in these extracts about what it is the job of MPs to represent? Are they justifiable in a modern democracy?

claim to represent. MPs such as George Gardiner have condemned this refusal to represent opinions, (see Box 1.2) but most MPs would argue that their decision protects the moral and security interests of the public by maintaining the reputation of the law and protecting innocents from execution, while denying martyrdom to terrorists. In January 2004, Labour MP Stephen Pound went back on a promise to promote a Private Members' Bill on a subject of the choosing of listeners to BBC Radio Four's *Today* programme after they opted for a law allowing householders to attack intruders to their homes. Pound dismissed the proposal as a 'ludicrous, brutal, unworkable blood-stained piece of legislation'. He went on to recall the catchphrase of defeated American state Senate candidate, Dick Tuck: 'The people have spoken – the bastards'. Other recent allegations of MPs' failure to represent the views of their constituents can be seen below under interpretation 4, 'Opinion'.

Interestingly, George Gardiner also exercised his independence as an MP by leaving the Conservative Party, in whose name he was elected, to join the Referendum Party in 1997, as three other Conservative MPs had done in the same Parliament (two to the Liberal Democrats and one to Labour). A further two Conservative MPs have done so since 1997, and two Labour MPs transferred to the Liberal Democrats during 2001–05. In 1981, twenty-nine Labour MPs and a Conservative defected to the SDP, but only one submitted himself to a by-election (and lost).

This is sometimes described as 'responsible' rather than as 'representative' government, in that it fails to represent short-term public opinion; even the most independently justified of such actions is usually defended in the end, however, by reference to its long-term recognition by the general public. Thus, while Mrs Thatcher refused to 'court public opinion' by reversing unpopular policies on interest rates and unemployment in her 1980 Conservative Party conference speech, the defence of this was sealed by her victory in the 1983 election and, indeed, by the Conservatives' subsequent victories at two further elections, following which the Labour Party adopted similar policies to win power. Conversely, Norman Lamont criticised John Major after leaving the latter's government in 1993, saying,

> there is something wrong with the way we make our decisions. The government listens too much to the pollsters and the party managers. The trouble is that they're not even very good at politics, and they are entering too much into policy decisions. As a result, there is too much short-termism, too much reacting to events, not enough shaping of events. We give the impression of being in office but not in power.

Similar criticisms were made of Tony Blair and his adviser Philip Gould, in July 2000 following leaks of memos in which they expressed fears that New Labour was perceived as 'out of touch'. Blair himself, however, adopted a different tone with the onset of the argument about how to tackle Iraq's failure to comply with United Nations weapons inspections. Pressing for the use of military force on the day over a million people demonstrated against war, the Prime Minister told a Labour Conference in Scotland: 'I do not seek unpopularity as a badge of honour. But sometimes it is the price of leadership and the cost of conviction.'

Advocates of this view of representation are suspicious of the sort of appeal to short-term public sentiment which has become known recently as 'dog whistle politics': the use of sharp, attention-grabbing messages. Thus, the Conservatives were criticised for opening their 2005 election campaign with billboards and leaflets offering a string of brief statements on issues such as law and order, immigration and public health, inviting voters to consider whether they were 'thinking what the Conservatives were thinking'. Critics regarded this as **populism**, that is to say, an appeal to ill-considered, simplistic reactions among the public which, while widespread, may be short lived or simply unwise. Responsible politicians, it was argued, should not manipulate and capitalise upon public misconceptions in this way. 'Populism', then, can be regarded as a concept which stigmatises public opinion where it is held to be in error, and suggests that it is not the job of representatives to put it into action. To put it another way, a French revolutionary once remarked that 'democracy is what we call the public when we agree with them'; populism is perhaps what a Burkean representative calls their opinions when he does not.

4 Opinion Modern politicians commonly argue that they are representing not only the interests of their constituents, but also the decisions those constituents would themselves take about their interests. In its purest form this is known as 'delegation', a **delegate** being one who is instructed to promote a certain opinion in an assembly or at a meeting, rather than exercising the judgement and discretion of a representative of interests in the style favoured by Burke. For this reason, the terms 'delegate' and 'representative' are often regarded as mutually exclusive alternatives although, of course, the latter does perform the act of representation.

Delegation is sometimes practised in trade unions and political parties, in which branches of the organisation will send their representatives to conferences with binding instructions upon how to vote on specific resolutions. This is also the defence adopted by many MPs when promoting either constituency claims and grievances or, if they wish – like the Eurosceptics of John Major's Conservative Party, or Labour MPs opposing welfare reforms under Blair – to defy their Party whip in support of what they claim are the views of their constituents. The following are more recent examples of attempts to voice public opinion against sitting MPs accused of misrepresenting their constituents:

- The Eurosceptic Referendum Party in 1997, and the UK Independence Party since then, have appealed to voters on the grounds that their anxieties about European integration have not been represented by the MPs of all parties who have supported the Single European Act, and the Treaties of Maastricht, Amsterdam and Nice;
- Independent MP Dr Richard Taylor won Wyre Forest in 2001 and held it in 2005 on a campaign to protect hospital services, over

which he said Labour had broken its promises to local constituents. Dr Taylor described his defeat of Junior Minister, David Lock, as 'a tremendous reaction from the people against a very powerful government, against a very powerful political system that overrides the will of the people';

- In 2005, 'Respect' candidate George Galloway ousted Labour's Oona King in Bethnal Green and Bow. King had supported the government's policy of war in Iraq, and Galloway argued that she had misrepresented the views of her constituents, 55,000 of whom were Bengali Muslims. Galloway promised that he would stand aside after one term in favour of a Bengali candidate (another example of the link between interpretations 2 and 4). Even a fierce critic of Galloway, such as the *Independent*'s Deborah Orr, could acknowledge that Oona King 'is certainly an example of a politician who followed her leader first and represented her constituents second'.

Even a relatively loyal Labour MP, such as Tony Clarke (Northampton South), feels it important to state that his proudest achievement in the 2001 Parliament was 'being a real constituency representative representing the views of constituents in parliament rather than representing parliament within the constituency', for instance by opposing the government over the war in Iraq and foundation hospitals. Indeed, the Labour governments since 1997 have responded to the demand for specific policy commitments with the use of pledge cards identifying specific promises with which Labour candidates associate themselves, a practice which has been adopted by other parties, too. This has produced a further difficulty, since contest then arises as to what opinion is being expressed by the vote: back-bench MPs claim that they know their constituents' views better than the government can; party whips reply that voters support candidates because of their party label and the opinions associated with it, and this obliges MPs to support that opinion even when they themselves disagree with it. On the day after the 2005 general election, Labour's campaign co-ordinator, Alan Milburn, reminded a *Channel Four News* reporter that 'what we've got is a radical, *New* Labour manifesto which everybody has signed up to: that is the basis on which everybody fought their campaign, so we know what we've got to deliver'.

Representation thus describes quite distinct relationships in different contexts although it is evident that, in British politics, elements of all of these interpretations are present in the work and the claims to authority of political leaders. In political theory, it has been the contention of many leftist writers and activists, from J.-J. Rousseau to C. B. Macpherson,[2] that genuine representation of one person by another is not possible or at least that, if necessary, must be strictly limited to delegation alone. Conservatives and Liberals, for different reasons, would argue that representation is not the same as democracy, but that this is part of its virtue rather than a weakness. The question of whether representation and democracy are separate abstract concepts, then, is not in dispute; the question of whether both can confer authority, however, and can coexist in a modern political system, is.

Liberty

Like representation, liberty is commonly associated with democracy; unlike representation, liberty is also a concept that is as universally claimed by political doctrines as democracy. Each tradition regards (or at least claims to regard) its distinctive conception of liberty as inextricably linked with the achievement of democracy; indeed, in each there is some conflation of the two terms that needs to be clarified if we are to make sense of our analysis. In fact, any definition of individual liberty will collide with a commitment to pure democracy at that point where the individual adopts a policy inconsistent with the declared view of the public, however expressed, and, in any arrangement or understanding of the concepts involved, this is clearly possible, not to say highly likely. The running together of these terms is therefore unhelpful; what is needed is an appreciation of the ways in which they have been modified so as to achieve (or attempt) an accommodation between them.

All mainstream British political ideologies distinguish between 'liberty' (legitimate freedom to pursue individual aims) and 'licence' (unrestrained freedom to do whatever the individual chooses). What separates the ideologies is their view of the conditions under which that freedom is best obtained, and the sorts of free action that are legitimate, and that have priority in the event of liberties competing or conflicting with one another. Three broad versions of the notion of liberty can be identified in modern politics.

Political liberty

Since the seventeenth century, liberalism been characterised by belief in basic liberties and rights within the political and legal framework of a country: free speech, freedom of thought and religion, association and assembly, fair public trial, property, government by consent, and more recently the right to vote. Liberal thinkers have always held that, without freedom to choose between ideas, parties, candidates and private actions, democracy is meaningless as an expression of the exercise of individual reason. Strengthening the constraints upon government required to protect these rights is still a distinctive concern of the Liberal Democrats, who favour electoral and parliamentary reform, the introduction of a bill of rights and devolution of power away from Westminster. Indeed, it was the threat to these and similar rights that caused veteran Labour MP, Brian Sedgemore, to defect to the Liberal Democrats during the 2005 general election campaign, saying 'if a political party does not yearn for freedom based on the rule of law, habeas corpus and due protest, then there is no point being a member of it or voting for it'. Though much of this agenda has become common currency among British parties, and basic political liberties have been a boast (even if a vain one) of the English political establishment for centuries, there remains a lively debate about the protection of civil liberties, illustrated by, for example, controversy over the use by the authorities of CCTV and identity cards, and the right to trial by jury. Such liberties, however, are not always consistent with pure democracy, as de Tocqueville recognised in his famous remark that 'some have not feared to assert that a people can never out step the boundaries of justice and reason. But that is the language of a slave.'

The principle of political liberalism is the rule of law rather than of men, and this may mean that the rights of unpopular minorities are protected against the wishes of the majority, as for instance when the age of consent for homosexual men was reduced in 1998 to the same as that for heterosexuals, thus protecting their privacy, but offending against majority opinion as expressed in public polls at the time. In the

United States the Supreme Court has performed this protective function for citizens, from pornographers and political extremists to the
gun lobby or black activists opposing discrimination; the incorporation of the European Convention on Human Rights into British law
has meant that British judges are drawn into a similar position of
defying (or at least of assessing) elected politicians or evident popular
opinion. It might, for example, have been difficult for the Home
Secretary to introduce the Prevention of Terrorism Act in 1974, or the
removal of Sinn Fein from public broadcasting in 1988, although
these were patently measures enjoying public (and in the case of the
former, cross-party) support. More recently, the Human Rights Act
has formed the basis of the House of Lords' judgment that indefinite
detention of foreign nationals under anti-terrorist law is contrary
to the Convention, and this has led to the introduction of so-called
'house arrest' procedures by Charles Clarke as Home Secretary. In the
wake of terrorist attacks upon the British public, the civil libertarian
may have difficulty giving the public the final say on whether identity
cards should be made compulsory in the United Kingdom, and, if so,
how the information stored upon them might be used. For the student
of democracy, the significance of these cases is not merely their details
in isolation, or even the way in which they relate to public opinion, but
more fundamentally the issue is: are there any freedoms and rights that
are beyond the legitimate reach of public opinion – that ought not to
be subject to majority approval? If there are, which ones are they,
and why are they the freedoms that are 'beyond democracy'? For political liberals, the protection of such a 'private sphere' is a fundamental purpose of the state, and the so-called 'tyranny of the majority' a
constant menace in a democratic society. The responses to these
difficulties, offered by thinkers such as Madison, de Tocqueville and
most of all J. S. Mill, are explored in Chapter 3.

Social liberty

With the emergence of New Liberalism and Socialism at the beginning of the twentieth century, a conception of liberty was developed
which took account of the material context of capitalism, and argued
that inequalities in wealth compromised the supposed right offered by
classical Liberalism. This is recognised in the writings of progressive

liberals such as L. T. Hobhouse and J. M. Keynes, and in the theory of '**positive freedom**' of philosophical figures such as Isaiah Berlin. The right to a fair trial, for example, means little if access to the law depends upon excessive legal fees; free speech is more available to those who own television stations and newspapers than to those who cannot read or write; and freedom to trade and own property, naturally, is more valuable to those who have the initial capital with which to invest. The rule of law is thus unequal in a society divided between classes, where, as Anatole France sneered, 'the law in its majestic equality forbids the rich as well as the poor to sleep under bridges, to beg in the streets, and to steal bread'. Shortly before his death in 1977, leading Labour cabinet minister and intellectual heavyweight, Anthony Crosland, reminded his younger colleague, Roy (now Lord) Hattersley, that democratic socialism 'is about the pursuit of equality and the protection of freedom – in the knowledge that until we are truly equal, we will not be truly free'.[3] Neil Kinnock articulated this critique of the *laissez-faire* view of liberty in a memorable speech used in a 1987 Labour Party election broadcast, responding to claims that, under the Conservatives, Britain was more 'free':

> I think of the youngsters I meet – three, four, five years out of school, never had a job, and they say to me: 'Do you think we'll ever get a job?' These are young men and women living in a free country, but they don't feel free. I think of the fifty-five-year-old woman I meet waiting months to go into hospital for an operation, her whole existence clouded by pain: she is a citizen of a free country, but she doesn't feel free.

The collectivist tradition regards provision of free welfare, progressive taxation and levelling of standards of living as a precondition of real freedom, and democracy may or may not help in that process. Provided that workers are numerous, conscious and well-organised enough to use the mechanisms of democracy to achieve these aims, then democracy and socialism will walk hand in hand. On coming into office as Chancellor, Gordon Brown said: 'What angers people is that millions are denied the opportunity to realise their potential and are powerless to do so. It is this inequality which must be addressed . . . and it is putting this into practice that is the central task of the Government.'[4] This was reflected in the New Deal programme to reduce youth unemployment, funded in part by the Windfall Tax on excess profits in privatised industries, and the introduction of the Minimum Wage.

More radical socialists believe the absence of freedom which capitalism entails may make the union between parliamentary democracy and equality at best difficult and at worst impossible, as appeared to be the case in the 1980s and 1990s, when the British public – often including the majority of the working class – proved repeatedly unwilling to vote for high taxation to fund public expenditure. Ironically, it might be argued that this was best proved by the emergence of New Labour, and its abandonment of the idea of equality of outcome. Even Roy Hattersley became sufficiently exasperated to write after the 2001 election that Labour was 'No longer my party', and that

> now my party not only pursues policies with which I disagree; its whole programme is based on a principle that I reject. One thing is clear: I cannot retain both membership and self respect unless I make apparent that much of what the Labour Party now proposes is wrong . . . At this moment Labour stands for very little that can be identified with social democracy. And the Prime Minister's adoption of what is essentially a free-for-all philosophy presents party members with a desperate choice.[5]

This dilemma was reflected at the 2005 general election by John Harris, a former Labour activist whose book *So Now Who do We Vote for?* argued that the Labour Party's conception of freedom had converged too closely with the Conservatives' free-market, economic one described below, and that he therefore suffered from 'the queasy feeling that comes from being cut adrift'.[6]

On the other hand, when put into practice, the collectivist approach can contradict some basic political and economic liberties that others regard as more important than social justice, and central to democracy – for instance, by the institution of the closed shop, requiring all workers in a firm or department to join a particular trade union, by punitive taxation which encroaches upon the property rights of high-income earners, or by the prohibition of private trade in education or health.

Economic liberty

Liberty for those on the Right – particularly the New Right – is much more clearly negative in character, that is to say, it is concerned with freedoms ensured by the inaction, rather than the action, of others, particularly the state. The concept of economic liberty is founded upon John Locke's premise that 'the first right was a right of property' and Adam Smith's principle of the 'Invisible Hand' of the market, and emphasises the right to own and trade in private property. These ideas were resuscitated and linked directly to democracy by Friedrich Hayek in *The Road to Serfdom* (1944)[7] and more recently in the United States by Robert Nozick in *Anarchy, State and Utopia* (1974)[8] and Milton Friedman in *Capitalism and Freedom* (1962)[9] and *Free to Choose* (1980).[10] In modern British politics, this has been reflected in the programme of 'rolling back the frontiers of the state' undertaken by the Thatcher administrations, and continued since under Major and Blair, including privatisation of large portions of state-owned industry and welfare services, such as council housing; targeting of other welfare benefits; and the reduction of direct taxation, as was promised in the Conservatives' most recent general election campaign. In the 1980s, Norman Tebbit demanded that 'we should be free to benefit from our efforts, free to engage in business, free to own our homes and to choose our children's schools'.[11] This view of liberty, alluded to in numerous Conservative general election slogans, such as 'Conservative Freedom Works', is conceived of by its adherents as inherently linked to the idea of '**property-owning democracy**', since it regards widely distributed private property as the best guarantee of protection from tyranny, and the exercise of consumer choice as a means of popular control, whether in the private sector or in market-driven state services such as education or health. This is what David Willetts referred to as 'an economic democracy in which we all vote with our pounds',[12] in which everything, from universities to railway companies, banks to burger bars or television stations, does the public's bidding to win custom.

Once again, this conception of liberty is at odds with the others above (seeing the state as a threat rather than as a protector or provider, for instance, and also presuming reasonably equal access to the pounds with which to 'vote'), and may – despite the claims of its

Box 1.3 Different conceptions of liberty

Source A: The Opportunity Society, Tony Blair's speech to the Labour Party Conference, 28 September 2004
'Sure, we're proud of our record. Record economic stability in the first term. Record investment in the second. Record numbers of jobs in both. A fairer Britain, yes. Better than Tory Britain, I should hope so. But not yet a Britain in which, as our Constitution puts it, "power, wealth and opportunity are in the hands of the many not the few". If you have professional parents you are five times more likely to go to university. If you live in a smart part of town you are half as likely to be the victim of crime. Company directors aren't the ones losing their pension. There is a glass ceiling on opportunity in this country. We have raised the ceiling. We haven't broken it.

For the wealthy few, every one of those challenges of the future can be overcome. The third-term mission is to overcome them for the many. The twentieth-century traditional welfare state that did so much for so many has to be reshaped as the opportunity society capable of liberation and advance every bit as substantial as the past but fitting the contours of the future. And this will be a progressive future as long as we remember that the reason for our struggle against injustice has always been to liberate the individual. The argument is not between those who do and those who do not love freedom. It is between the Conservatives who believe freedom requires only that Government stand back while the fittest and most privileged prosper. And we who understand, that freedom for the individual, for every individual, whatever their starting point in life, is best achieved through a just society and a strong community.'

Source B: The Real Alternative, Liberal Democrat manifesto, April 2005

'Our Principles
Freedom. Fairness. Trust. These are the qualities of the British people at their best, and they are the guiding principles of the Liberal Democrats. This manifesto is built on these principles – principles that we believe must underpin the government of this country, but which are too often lacking in public life today.

Freedom – because Liberal Democrats believe that individuals should govern their own lives, free from unnecessary interference by government or society. So we want to build a society which gives individual men and women opportunities to pursue their aims, develop their talents and shape their successes. A country where people are free to shape their future is stronger, wealthier, happier, and more fulfilled.

This Government just keeps trying to take away citizens' basic freedoms – such as the right to jury trial, or to demonstrate peacefully outside parliament. They even wanted the power to lock anyone up at the whim of the Home Secretary. They plan to charge every citizen nearly £100 each to hold a compulsory identity card, despite the fact that other countries have found that they don't work. It's all done in the name of cutting crime and tackling terrorism; but it is the terrorists who want to take away freedom and democracy – our government should defend our liberties.'

Source C: Conservative Party website, 2005 (www.conservatives. com/tile.do?def=party.beliefs.page)

'Personal Freedom
Conservatives believe the people should be big, and the state should be small. That is why we are determined to thin down Labour's fat government. Today Labour's bloated bureaucracy is the same size as the population of Sheffield – and there are more civil servants in the Department of Work and Pensions than there are soldiers in the British Army. We will freeze civil service recruitment and reduce the mountain of regulations which Labour has inflicted on Britain – its businesses, its education service and its NHS.

Enterprise and Opportunity
Conservatives believe that personal happiness and economic success alike flourish when individuals and families are free to seize opportunities in their own way. It is the task of government to increase opportunities and remove barriers to them. Above all, we believe in the benefits of low taxes. It is right that people keep more of what is theirs – because it leads to greater economic success that benefits everyone.

Choice
Conservatives believe that people need choice to exercise responsibility – which is the hallmark of a free society. Putting choice directly in the hands of parents and patients means that funding for schools and hospitals goes straight to the front line – and drives improvements in quality.'

All the main political parties are talking the language of freedom: is that because they agree with each other, or because they mean different things by it?

proponents – sit ill with democracy. If the majority votes for state provision, or high taxation, the rights of property must for libertarians prevail, as, in the slogan used by followers of the American 'Moral Majority' pressure group, the purest form of this tradition argues that 'taxation is theft'. In other, less spectacular cases, pensioners have recently refused to pay Council Tax bills they regarded as excessive. The common theme is that the right to property supersedes – indeed precedes – any decision at the ballot box.

What you should have learnt from reading this chapter

- There is sufficient common ground among the main British political parties about these questions to ensure that the tensions identified above rarely produce major conflicts. All pay at least lip service to basic political rights, to some level of free education and health provision, and to the context of a capitalist, market-oriented society.

- This does not obscure the fact that each tradition of liberty is at odds with the other, claims a uniquely close relationship with democracy, and at the same time holds that ultimately democracy must come second to its own notion of rights in the event of the two being mutually exclusive.

- What the material in this chapter indicates is that, while we are used to rolling representation, liberty and democracy together in the same breath, the titles 'representative democracy' and 'liberal democracy' are in some respects each a contradiction in terms.

- Indeed, while modern democracies almost all seek to avoid the potential dilemmas and tensions involved, the earliest form of democracy made no pretence of doing so. The journey from that system to the present day is the subject of the next chapter.

Glossary of key terms

Civil liberty One of those freedoms enjoyed as a matter of principle by all full members of a society, such as freedom of speech, equal access to the law, or the right to vote.

Delegate One who is obliged to act upon the exact policies and opinions of the larger body he or she represents, rather than simply a perception of their best interests.

Populism An appeal to popular sentiment and sympathy which is made simply to win support rather than to seek a just or wise policy.

Positive freedoms Freedoms, enjoyment of which may require action by the state or some other outside body, such as the rights to work, to an education or to health care.

Property-owning democracy A society in which power is spread equally because capital – in the form of shares, housing or other significant property – is privately owned but increasingly equally accessible to (but not equally shared by) all.

Social representation The practice of copying in an institution the chief social characteristics of the population it governs, such as the proportions of men and women, ethnic groups and age profile.

Likely examination questions

Is democracy possible without economic and social equality?

To what extent is liberal democracy a contradiction in terms?

'Our view of how democracy best works is largely a reflection of our view of human nature.' Discuss.

Helpful websites

Examples of current campaigns to improve ethnic minority and female representation in British politics can be found at www.obv.org.uk/info/welcome.html (Operation Black Vote) and www.fawcettsociety.org.uk/ (The Fawcett Society).

Competing liberal, socialist and conservative conceptions of freedom can be seen reflected at the websites of the Campaign for Freedom of Information (www.cfoi.org.uk/) and Liberty (www.liberty-human-rights.org.uk/); the TUC Workers' Rights site (www.tuc.org.uk/tuc/rights_main.cfm); and the Freedom Association (www.tfa.net/). It should be stressed, however, that these are not party organisations, but rather they reflect the three ideological traditions.

Suggestions for further reading

The first of these explores the abstract political concepts surrounding representation, while the second sets them in their practical context:

Hanna Pitkin, *The Concept of Representation* (University of California Press, 1972).

David Judge, *Representation: Theory and Practice in Britain* (Routledge, 1999).

The following all examine the relationship between the three main political traditions and the ideas of freedom and representative democracy – some from a more partisan standpoint than others:

Edmund Dell, *A Strange Eventful History: Democratic Socialism in Britain* (HarperCollins, 2000).

Roy Hattersley, *Choose Freedom: The Future of Democratic Socialism* (Penguin, 1987).

Andrew Heywood, 'Liberal Democracy', *Talking Politics*, vol. 3, No. 2, winter 1990–1.

Kevin Hickson, *The Political Thought of the Conservative Party since 1945* (Palgrave Macmillan, 2005).

Barry Holden, *Understanding Liberal Democracy* (Prentice Hall, 1993).

David Willetts, *Modern Conservatism* (Penguin, 1992).

The Origins of Democracy

Contents

Overview

We owe the invention of the name – and perhaps the values – of democracy to the people of classical Greece. The origins of democracy in the city-state of Athens in the fifth century BC illustrate some of the fundamental problems of the concept, but are in other ways quite distinct from all modern forms. The Athenian system is a compelling example of the way in which an historical reality provides an idea that becomes the kernel of a great myth, which then acts as the seed of almost endless political ideas and actions in our own time. What is important here is not so much the detailed mechanics of the system, but the philosophy of power supposedly underpinning classical democracy, and the impact of those values on the popular political consciousness.

Key issues to be covered in this chapter

- What were the key features of Athenian democracy?
- How did the society of ancient Athens affect the operation of the democracy?
- What were the system's strengths?
- What were the system's weaknesses?
- What elements of the system, if any, are retained in modem democracies such as Britain?
- Could the spirit of Athenian democracy usefully be restored in modern Britain?

Athenian democracy

Although the dates and locations of the first experiments in popular rule are matters of fierce historical dispute, there has been consensus about Athens as the earliest sustained and fully documented example of such a system, to the extent that it has taken on a mythical and idealistic character in retrospect. Athens is remembered fondly by political theorists for the fact that, for most of the period from 508 BC to 322 BC, the city was run by an assembly or *Ecclesia* consisting of the entire citizenry of 40,000 men who voted directly on legislation, and personally held accountable officials, most of whom gained their posts for short periods by **sortition**, or lot, rather like modern jurors. Positions open only to certain **citizens** – involving military expertise or financial backing – were elected by, and answerable to, the citizenry and, in some cases, those in charge had to settle state debts for which they had made the city liable. This was democracy without representation: the sovereign body was the electorate, and citizens of Ancient Athens gave up days at a time, forty times a year, to participate in a system that boasted of its *isegoria* (equal right of speech) and *isonomia* (equal political rights) as well as its *demokratia* (rule of the *demos*, or 'people'). As often as possible, decisions were made by *homonoia* or unanimity but, where necessary, a vote of all citizens present was taken.

Not all the features were retained throughout the period of the democracy but, politically, Athens is more important as a symbol or myth than as an historical reality. It is to the notion of 'pure' original democracy of classical times that writers and activists of recent generations have repeatedly turned for inspiration – to the idea of a community that governs itself, that exercises power with the authority of a popular mandate, rather than being governed by a smaller, self-interested group of people. To recent activists, Athens symbolised the principle that participation is the authentic means of legitimating laws, as well as being an 'improving' civic duty. Democracy, idealistically, was presumed to grant true freedom because those who obeyed the law (although this is a somewhat misleading term because, to the Greeks, 'law' referred to the more fundamental and static rules of political activity) made it: the characteristic feature of democracy was that it distributed power equally among all those over whom it was exercised.

'Ruling and being ruled in turn', Aristotle wrote, 'is one element in liberty'; Pericles' funeral oration famously boasted that 'we do not say that a man who takes no interest in politics is a man who minds his own business; we say he has no business here at all'. While the historical details of Athens are secondary here, two observations are relevant because they recur throughout the debate about democracy:

1 Athenian democracy had both problems and critics;
2 Most forms of democracy in the modern world have differed radically from that of classical times, and – despite their architects' pretensions – were deliberately intended to do so.

The problems with democracy

A substantial and prestigious body of thought in Athens, both during and after the democratic regime, regarded democracy as 'acknowledged folly', as Alcibiades put it. Critics of democracy pointed to four principal flaws inherent in, or at least consequent upon, democratic rule which can still be recognized today:

1. Democracy supposes people to be equal when they are not. Plato was the keenest advocate of this argument that, merely being subject to the law, was not a qualification for making it. He compared public opinion to 'a large and powerful animal', with no inherent sense of morality nor any means of communicating anything other than base tastes to its master, in whose role Plato cast the democratic politician: 'He would not really know which of the creature's tastes and desires was admirable or shameful, good or bad, right or wrong; he would simply use the terms on the basis of its reactions, calling what pleased it good, what annoyed it bad.' Interestingly, the animal theme frequently characterises criticisms of populist politics today, as with the concept of 'dog-whistle'(superficial, attention-grabbing) issues; one researcher at MORI recently even described public opinion as having the clumsy reactions of 'an eight-hundred-pound gorilla'. What great music or poetry, Plato asks, was ever discovered by turning to popular opinion for judgement? What great leadership, therefore, can be expected from appealing to the tastes of a public which is at best only grudgingly interested and poorly informed?

Elsewhere in *The Republic*, Plato compares the democratic state to a ship on which the crew are divided among themselves about what to do because the captain is proving inadequate. They split into factions, which engage in intrigue and intimidation to gain control of the helm, but none of the contenders is as skilled even as the old captain; one figure on board is entirely ignored – that of the truly able navigator, who can read the stars and handle the ship, but alternately bores and depresses the crew with accounts of the work necessary to run the ship successfully, and realistic but unimpressive prospects of travel. This weakness of democracy was recognised by politicians of all parties in a discussion about the causes of political alienation in which Charles Kennedy acknowledged that:

> Politicians are to blame . . . because they do raise unreasonable expectations . . . The great difficulty . . . is you can't go into the next general election . . . and say 'Vote for us and we will manage your decline more competently than the other lot can.' You have got to sell your activists hope, you've got to sell the public hope if they're going to come and vote for you.[1]

Plato's able navigator represents the figure of the Philosopher King, whom Plato saw as representing true worth in society, but whom democratic societies shun in favour of shallow, emotive orators, or *rhetores* as they were known in Athens, who came and went with public whims, and never resolved problems justly, but generated resentment at their failure to fulfil unrealistic promises. This criticism is the starting-point of the modern Élitist tradition of political analysis (see Chapter 3) which sees leadership as a specialised activity, requiring natural talent not always recognisable by ordinary citizens, if not also lengthy training.

2. Democracy encourages too great a presumption of individual freedom, and this strikes at the common values and customs of society. By asserting that one person's opinion is as good as another's, democracy fostered a fragmented and potentially unstable society, without respect for tradition or established institutions. Isocrates condemned the idea that 'as soon as they reached man's estate', citizens 'were allowed to do what they liked'; Aristotle thought it bad that each person lived 'according to his fancy'; and

Plato reported with horror that 'the city is full of liberty and free speech and everyone in it is allowed to do what he likes'. This fear of moral and social **relativism** is commonly reiterated in modern Conservative thought from Edmund Burke onwards: de Tocqueville wrote in *Democracy in America* that the system 'not only makes each man forget his forefathers, but it conceals him from his descendants and separates him from his contemporaries; it ceaselessly throws him back on himself alone and threatens finally to confine him entirely in the solitude of his own heart'. A modern conservative commentator like Professor Roger Scruton can point approvingly to these sentiments, and reiterate the warning that 'there is a great danger that democracy produces the habit of questioning everything'.[2]

Box 2.1 Three Greek doubters

Though the Delphic Oracle declared him the wisest man in the world, **Socrates** (before 469–399 BC) wrote no surviving works. He was the teacher of Plato (427–347 BC) who used him as a mouthpiece in many of his critical accounts of democracy. Socrates believed that truth was discovered by the clash of contrary facts and ideas, and lived by the principle that virtue lies in knowledge. Condemned by the Athenian authorities for his teachings, he insisted on receiving the death penalty, and drank hemlock.

Socrates' pupil, **Plato** left much clearer evidence of his criticisms of Athenian democracy: in his many works, notably *The Republic*, and in his teachings at the Academy, which he established in 388 BC, Plato argued that the ideal society was one based upon a rigid class structure made up of guardians, military and workers. He believed that truth was to be found by 'Philosopher Kings' trained from youth to rule in search of the 'forms', universal and timeless truths incomprehensible to ordinary men.

Plato in turn taught **Aristotle** (384–322 BC), who acknowledged his teacher's recognition of natural inequality, and who was concerned about the impact of democracy on the rule of law. He departed from Platonism after his teacher's death, however, and argued that some decisions could be made better by a large number of poorer minds than by a small group of remote experts. Aristotle nonetheless retained a belief that there is a natural order in which we have a distinct position, and his ideal form of government was a broad-based oligarchy.

3. The purest forms of democracy disrupt the rule of law, and thus make possible arbitrary government. Though generally an admirer of democratic principles, Aristotle believed that they were only part of the best sort of constitution because, without some sort of constraint, in the Athenian system, 'the mass of the people (or the "majority") is sovereign, instead of the law'. Those Greek philosophers, who regarded the law as an immutable (if limited) set of universally recognised principles within which democratic decisions were best made, anticipate concerns voiced later. Conservative and liberal writers (for different reasons) have been anxious that a capricious and ill-informed mass might override the established conventions of politics, such as freedom of speech and belief, fair trial, equality before the law, and redress of grievances against the state: in their view, these commanded a higher authority than mere numbers of voters. Aristotle may have had in mind the infamous execution of Socrates by the Athenian democracy in 399 BC for the crime of being 'a curious person, searching into things under the earth and above the heaven: and making the worse appear the better cause, and teaching all this to others'. It is here that the notion of 'totalitarian' or 'despotic' democracy – a democratic regime that infringes upon liberal conceptions of civil liberties – emerges, one which was used by critics of the French Revolution, such as Alexis de Tocqueville, in conjuring up the idea of a 'Tyranny of the majority': 'Some have not feared to assert that a people can never out step the boundaries of justice and reason in those affairs which are peculiarly its own; and that consequently full power may be given to the majority by which they are represented. But that is the language of a slave.'

4. Democracy encourages the emergence of factions which tyrannise their opponents once in control of the sovereign body. The problem of uninhibited popular rule became still more worrying when it became obvious that any group capturing a temporary majority in the Assembly could then exercise the full power of the state in its own private interest – and a key assertion of critics of democracy has always been that popular decision-making does not produce popular consensus or a common sense of identity. Most obvious was the division of interest between the rich and the poor, and the classical writer known as 'The Old Oligarch' is among the earliest of a tradition who saw democracy merely as a weapon for punishing the propertied, and any other minority, religious, cultural or regional, under the guise of the magical force of popular opinion. Indeed, the very term '*demos*' is often taken to refer to a social class, the poor, or the 'mob', rather than to a technical class of citizen. Plato claimed that 'democracy results when the poor defeat the others and kill or expel them', and Aristotle argued 'the real point of difference is poverty and wealth . . . and where the poor rule, it is democracy'.

Certainly Athens's citizenry was divided into recognisable classes – of whom the *Pentekosimedimnoi* were the richest, and others split into military groups – and tribes, each with distinctive agendas and interests. Indeed, it has been argued that one of the more dangerous achievements of the lawgiver Solon was to divorce the ideas of political and economic democracy from each other. This view is reflected in modern writers both sceptical and supportive of democracy: James Madison, a 'Protective' democrat, who wanted to introduce democratic principles into the American Constitution chiefly to limit state power, was determined to restrain the influence of 'factions', or self-interested groups, within the system, which he regarded as an inevitable element of political debate; revolutionary Leftists, such as Lenin, on the other hand, have approved the idea of democracy as an economic proposition. 'Alongside an immense expansion of democracy', he wrote, 'which for the first time becomes democracy for the poor, democracy for the people, and not for the moneybags, the dictatorship of the proletariat brings about a series of restrictions on the freedom of the oppressors, the exploiters, the capitalists.' Already, we can see that, what some regarded as strengths in democracy, others have always perceived as threats.

Differences between classical and modern democracy

If certain arguments about abstract themes in democracy have been repeated in ancient and modern politics, the differences between the circumstances and structures of the two versions are enormous, and must be borne in mind, especially by those seeking to draw comparisons, whether favourable or not. A series of features illustrate this divergence (see Box 1.3).

1. The electorate. Although all male citizens could vote in Athens, this included only about one in five of the city-state's population. Slaves, foreigners and women were excluded from the Assembly, and the granting of new citizenships was a major ceremony involving at least 6,000 citizens. Some have sought to argue that only under these conditions could attendance be practicable, although it is wrong to perceive slaves as uniformly involved in labour-intensive work, while their owners flitted from political discussion to performances of Sophocles' plays. Nonetheless, the possibility of granting an effective paid bank holiday to all adult citizens of Britain in order to come to any major policy decision does raise difficult logistical questions. Direct participation, if it involves all adults, would be physically difficult in communities larger than the Athenian city-state. A rare example is the system of local-government cantons in Switzerland.

2. Voting. Votes, when taken, were direct and open. Thus, not only did citizens take decisions and hold officials accountable in person, rather than through representatives, but they did so without the benefit of the secret ballot, a relatively recent invention, but one which most twentieth-century writers regard as integral to democracy, as the means by which to prevent intimidation and bribery.

Thus, the concept of democracy in its earliest form had only one central likeness with the forms commonly recognised today: the idea that power should be exercised by, or at least be accountable to, all those exposed to its use, and that this was the key moral source of authority, because all voters were regarded as having equal claim to govern their own lives. Whether or not these were genuine beliefs of the Greeks, or were the reasons that democracy was established, are less important here than the fact that these ideas were summoned by writers two thousand years later to justify a variety of modifications of democracy. Like classical scholars G. C. Field, Paul Cartledge and Benjamin Farrington, that most commentators have concluded 'the **Parliamentary governments** of Western Europe are certainly very unlike the Greek democracies, and a Greek democrat would hardly concede them the right to the name without very considerable qualifications';[3] that 'we are far from living in a system even vaguely resembling classical Athens',[4] and that 'we possess the name of democracy without the reality'.[5]

Could the principles and processes of Athenian democracy be revived in modern society?

After the passage of two-and-a-half millenniums, it might be exciting to be able to restore the ancient idea of citizenship using the most modern technology. This hope that the information and communication technology of the twenty-first century will be able to revive **direct democracy** has been expressed across the political spectrum for over a decade now. In particular, it has been argued that digital broadcasting and the Internet make possible – even perhaps appealing – the mass participation which has seemed simply impractical in mass society. In the late 1980s, Anthony Arblaster expressed optimism that 'modern means of communication . . . could easily overcome the isolation of any particular local assembly . . . It would even be possible for people to watch a political or parliamentary debate at home on television, and then register their vote or opinion at the end by pressing a button or making a phone call';[6] by 1994, a paper published by left-wing think tank, Demos, argued for 'a more participative, responsible democracy that will use the new technologies of push-button democracy and the electronic town hall'.[7] Meanwhile, on the Right, Paul Johnson claimed that, as a member of the British Cable Authority, he had seen from the 'immense, almost limitless possibilities of fibre-optic cables, that a new chapter in political democracy was opening', and hoped that the nation might sit down together every Friday night to resolve important public issues in a sort of giant political chat-room.[8] The developments in communications since then would appear to confirm those expectations: whereas in 1990 only 100,000 computers worldwide were connected to the Internet, the figure was 36 million, used by 150 million people, in 1998, and by 2004, over 800 million people were using on-line facilities. In February 2000, President Clinton's political consultant, Dick Morris, told the BBC's *On the Record* that, ultimately, 'the Internet will completely take over politics and the locus of political campaigning will shift from television to the Internet'; two months later, a Microsoft representative boasted on the Radio Four *Today* programme that 'the Internet will be everything to everyone'.

Political information has certainly become more accessible via these media: in Britain, cable, satellite and digital broadcasting has allowed the development of twenty-four-hour news and specialist channels covering parliamentary developments (BBC Parliament started with the slogan 'Democracy in Action'). The potential impact of Internet use, however, is dramatically different because of the relative ease with which smaller parties and campaigns can establish websites, the facility of the Net for focusing and filtering information for particular audiences, and the speed with which it can adapt its content. Though still a long way behind their American counterparts in both the quantity and sophistication of their use of the Internet, all British parties, and most MPs, have websites, often targeting particular issues and voters. In addition, there is a growing number of independent election websites and search engines linking thousands of party and political websites throughout the world. The global potential of this facility for the split-second transfer of vast bodies of information among millions of people worldwide first became evident in the role played by 'virtual democracy' (as such use of the Internet was already becoming known) in extending participation by delegates and pressure groups preparing for the 1995 United Nations Conference on Women at Beijing. More recently, at the last two British general elections, websites have sought to inform voters seeking to vote tactically to defeat the Conservatives. Frances Cairncross, Media Editor of *The Economist*, predicted ten years ago that 'circulating information will become faster; airing a view will be easier; mounting a campaign will be cheaper'. That process is surely not yet complete.

New technology goes further than mere receipt of information, however, and makes possible responses by voters: 'interactive' television debates followed by telephone or cable-based polls have been in use in Britain for over twenty years on questions ranging from the Reagan–Gorbachev summit of 1985 to the merits of comedians on talent shows, and most numerously, in terms of the two-and-a half million viewers involved in the poll, the future of the monarchy, in January 1997. This followed a televised debate, *Monarchy – The Nation Decides*, in which constitutional luminaries, such as night-club owner Peter Stringfellow and thriller writer Frederick Forsyth, answered questions from the audience on the issue. Telephone polls have also been used by some local councils in recent years to gauge public opinion on sensitive issues. The Internet allows the public to participate by making contributions to campaign funds, (the most common form of response encouraged by such sites in the United States) by asking politicians questions on-line, and most importantly by voting. Thus, the obvious practical objection to mass participation in a society of millions of voters has been, and is increasingly being, overcome to create what United States Vice-President Al Gore hailed in the 1990s as 'a new Athenian age of democracy'. British ministers, too, have been caught up in this atmosphere of excitement: after only 24 per cent of the electorate turned out for European Parliament elections in 1999, Home Office minister George Howarth announced plans for pilots in e-voting, saying 'voting procedures need to be brought in line with modern lifestyles. As services for consumers have changed, voting arrangements have stood still.' Robin Cook addressed a conference in April 2002 staged by the polling organisation, YouGov, which carries out its surveys through the Net, and which was already establishing itself with a reputation for rapid and reliable monitoring of public opinion in a field that had become discredited since the errors of polls ten years earlier. Cook said 'the Internet offers us a tool for participation without precedent in democratic history'. His successor as Leader of the Commons, Geoff Hoon, reiterated the point in July 2005.

The government has sponsored a number of trials of electronic political participation, including electronic surgeries, petitioning, and voting. These and other experiments run by the parties seem to show

---

Box 2.2 Geoff Hoon on electronic voting (July 2005)

It may seem strange to us – all of us so well versed in the political process – but I have met people who are intimidated at the prospect of entering a polling station because they are not sure how to vote – in the same way that that some people do not know how to place a bet in a bookmakers. New technology will certainly have a part to play . . . Millions vote using text messages in the reality TV shows that sometimes seem to dominate our television screens. Would it really be such a huge step to extend this option to voting in General Elections? . . . Electronic voting is an issue that demands further examination'.[9]

evidence of success in the processes of circulating information and posing questions, but the first extensive pilot of e-voting (in 2003) showed no significant increase in turn-out, according to the Electoral Commission.

There is a flavour of schoolboy imagination and excitement to much of the science-fiction talk surrounding these projects, and more recent experience has confirmed that there are good reasons to resist such euphoria. E-democracy has two sorts of problem: new ones associated with technology; and old, familiar ones visible in democracy as far back as Ancient Athens.

Technological problems

Access to the resources necessary for such decision-making is profoundly unequal. To make referendums more than a very periodic event in politics, we would need to use technology available only to some at present, such as the Internet, to which barely half of Britons currently have regular access, and of which perhaps fewer still have a full working knowledge. Although this figure will increase, it is unlikely at any time to be universal, and the ability to build websites and retrieve information will never be equally shared. There will always be an aristocracy of expertise in technology. After all, even the telephone and television do not reach all households.

An extensive study by Chris Barnes and Kester Isaac-Henry of the potential for using new technology in local government discovered that while – even among some 'hard-to-reach' or socially excluded groups – there was a reassuringly positive attitude towards, and awareness of, information and communication technology, 'the greater need would seem to be a substantial investment in information hardware and software and in the development of citizen skills'. Though they found over two-thirds of their respondents used information technology 'very often', fewer than a quarter of these used the Internet.[10] A report from the Parliamentary Office of Science and Technology concluded in 1998 that 'if the government wishes to replace existing paper-based interactions, it will need to do more than just put information and services on the Web, and ensure that other means of access are available'.[11] Since then, of course, Internet access and the uses to which it can be put have multiplied enormously but, in February 2005, the Office for National Statistics found that while for the first time over half of British households had an Internet connection, still 35 per cent of the population had never used the Internet, and 19 per cent agreed with the statement 'I have not really considered using the Internet before and I am not likely to in the future'. E-democracy tends to be most popular among those people most familiar with the technology involved – but they are in many cases an undemocratic minority, mostly already disproportionately powerful through education and income.

The new technology also brings with it problems of security and practical reliability which ballot-boxes and paper votes rarely present – at least when the conventional polling station rather than postal voting is used. The government has experimented enthusiastically with systems to allow voting via the Internet, and promises 'an e-enabled election some time after 2006'. Studies from the United States, however, have shown how electronic voting records can be lost or tampered with remotely and imperceptibly, sufficiently significantly as to affect the results. Former Environment Minister, Michael Meacher, warned in 2005 that 'e-voting is neither secure nor tamper-proof' and that 'we must be extremely cautious of the surge towards electronic voting . . . There are better ways of increasing turn-out than simply changing the voting technology.'[12] Most communications revolutions are hailed as heralding a rebirth of democracy, but each – like video, television, radio and cinema – suffers from too many practical weaknesses to function as a fundamentally new vehicle of public opinion.

Democratic problems

Even if we were to find a universally accessible medium of communication and voting, the problems associated with mass participation, which were feared by sceptics in Athens, would merely reappear in a more modern context. Moreover, e-democracy is not the face-to-face 'horizontal' discussion that the Athenians engaged in – it is a far more remote, momentary experience. Even a sympathetic analyst of the Athenian system, such as Benjamin Barber, has pointed out that 'you have to *learn* to be a citizen . . . By the middle of the Fifth Century in Athens, the Athenians had a hundred years of experience of talk, debate, dialogue.'[13] Problems of apathy, ignorance and volatility; of contest between different publics, or between majority opinion and minority rights, would all persist. As we saw in Chapter 2, these problems were raised by Plato and the other Athenian critics, and they were immediately recognised at the re-emergence of democracy in the Enlightenment, as we shall see in Chapter 3. Indeed, the speed with which decisions could be made would tend to exacerbate such problems. To illustrate, we need only turn to the Spanish election of March 2004, which might have had a very different result if held immediately following the Madrid bombings (when Spanish government ministers suggested Basque terrorist group ETA may have been responsible), instead of four days later when a clear link with the government's policy in Iraq had been established.

None of the attempts at reviving direct democracy using modern technology has (so far at any rate) altered the fundamental merits and problems of democracy, which arise from the merits and weaknesses of humans and their relations with one another. Whether we think democracy works or fails is at root a question of where we believe authority lies and, while new machines can service that dynamic debate with more information, and may help create the circumstances in which we were always hopeful democracy would work, our view of its limitations and potential never changes. Early on in the process of development of information technology, some seasoned analysts warned of what Professor John Gray called the 'illusion . . . that technology can succeed in emancipating human beings from poverty or isolation where political practice has failed'.[14] Twenty years ago electoral observer, Iain McLean, concluded of attempts to use computers for public votes that 'new technology can do things which used to be physically impossible. But it cannot achieve the logically impossible, and it does not relieve us of the need to think about the age-old disputes of political theory. We have technology which Plato, Rousseau and Mill never dreamed of; but we have not settled the arguments amongst them.'[15] Nor will we.

Box 2.3 The possibilities of e-democracy

Source A: The Economist, *17 June 1995*
'Here is the nightmare. A country, having succumbed to the lure of electronic democracy, and duly wired its voters into the Internet, decides that it will henceforth make its laws by letting anybody who so desires send a proposal into the information highway, after which every adult citizen will be invited to vote on these ideas, each Saturday evening. On Friday night a race riot in, say, Bradford – or Buffalo or Beziers or Bochum – kills half a dozen white people. The Internet hums, the e-mail crackles. Zap comes next day's empurpled answer: out with all Pakistanis/Hispanics/Algerians/Turks. And here is the rose-tinted dream. The people's elected representatives, having yet again failed to balance the budget, suddenly realise that the sensible thing to do is to put the problem to the people themselves. All the various possibilities are electronically presented to the voters. The voters express their assorted preferences. The contradictions in their answers are laid out for their further examination. They vote again. After a couple of months or so of furrowed-brow button-pressing, bingo, a budget virtuously balanced to the majority's satisfaction. Neither nightmare nor dream is likely to become reality. Most ordinary men and women are probably not foolish enough to risk the first or technologically arrogant enough to believe they can manage the second. Yet between these extremes of what technology might do to politics lies some fascinating new territory, well worth exploring.'

Source B: The Guardian, *4 February 1999*
' "If Ronald Reagan was the made-for-TV candidate, Jesse Ventura is the made-for-Net candidate", says Steven Clift. Bespectacled Clift does not seem a natural supporter of the flamboyant Ventura, the former pro wrestler who crushed the opposition in November's election for the Governorship of Minnesota. Where their interests coincide is in putting politics on the Web. Ventura's low-budget campaign made extensive use of the Internet to mobilise volunteers and communicate with voters and the media. In 1991, Clift pioneered teledemocracy. As a graduate working on citizen participation in politics, he concluded the Net would be "the most powerful medium in politics" and set up PUBPOL-L, the first public policy e-mail list. But his latest trip to Britain has not impressed him. He says the Net's democratic potential is being stifled in the UK by the high price of tele-communications. "As long as you have local call charges for the Net, citizen use from the home will be virtually impossible.

Democracy is inherently inefficient – participation is not about efficiency, it's about effectiveness, which often means investing time." '

Source C: Ivan Horrocks and Dominic Wring, 'The Myth of e-thenian Democracy', Politics Review, April 2001
'Perhaps the most visible example of why seeking a technological fix for the democratic crises is problematic occurred on the same day as the 2000 local elections. An event that vied with the results for the news headlines, the arrival of the 'I love You' virus, threw computer networks into disarray . . . There are more fundamental objections to the e-thenian model, however. The new technology could, in fact, undermine the existing democratic process by compounding existing biases in the distribution of knowledge and information; by fragmenting discourse between increasingly differentiated policy areas; and by reducing participation to a distant and marginalized vote in a knee-jerk reaction to a limited number of sound bite options . . . It is possible to conclude, therefore, that while it is clear that the new technology can assist in addressing some of the problems associated with the processes of democracy, such as voting, the possibilities of applying a technological fix to the underlying problems of democracy are far more questionable.'

Source D: Matthew Tempest and Martin Nicholls, 'E-vote early, e-vote often?' The Guardian, 17 April 2003
'Contain yourselves, but more people will have more ways of voting in England's May 1 local elections than ever before. Mobile phones, digital TV, postal voting and that ubiquitous holy grail, the 'worldwide interweb', will be at the disposal of a total of 6.5 million voters this year, taking Britain (or at least England) further away from what Robin Cook described as the "anachronism" of the pencil stub, and closer to the government's stated ambition of an e-enabled general election some time after 2006. The local government minister, Nick Raynsford, last week unveiled the 17 e-voting pilot schemes taking place, covering 1.4 million people, plus another 42 authorities which are piloting all-postal elections and other innovations.

The scheme builds on last year's May elections and mayoral referendums which saw 30 pilot schemes covering 2.5 million voters, although only all-postal voting showed a noticeable increase in voter turnout. And even that was variable, with Hackney – the fourth most deprived borough in the country and one of the worst performing according to government league tables – actually registering a 4% drop in turnout last May despite an all-postal vote. But as the small print to Mr Raynsford's press release makes clear, the ostensible aim of the exercise is to get more crosses in more boxes, so to speak.

'The document states: "The electoral pilot aims to improve turnout generally, in particular amongst key groups of people who might otherwise be excluded, e.g. people who are working away from the area, younger voters, the elderly and people with mobility problems." However, many within the IT industry are doubtful whether the issue can be solved by e-enablement. Common sense alone must force one to wonder whether it is really easier to register to vote by text message – which involves receiving for a four-digit PIN, then returning a choice of four, six or even eight candidates – than it is to stop in at the local primary school for the old-school plywood cubicle experience.'

Source E: Ross Ferguson, 'Diving in the Shallow End', in Stephen Coleman and Stephen Ward (eds), Spinning the Web: Online campaigning in the 2005 General Election, Hansard Society 2005
'It is easy to be negative about what was achieved through the online campaigning carried out by the candidates and parties in 2005. However, the short life-span of an election ties parties into zealously-choreographed campaigns, where they are restricted to the kind of political marketing that is criticised in the "everyday" parliamentary cycle. The positive aspect of the 2005 online election campaign is that MPs and other elected representatives gained first-hand experience of e-democracy's potential to help them "listen and learn". They witnessed the way in which the creative approaches and consensual discourse of e-democracy can motivate and lift the spirits of the electorate.

Through their use of blogs, they experienced a new potential for networking and scrutiny. Their use of deliberative platforms showed them how easy it is to carry out consultation. Back-end IT systems helped them to tap into rich seams of data. Taken together all this information showed elected representatives how to carry out their mandate in a much more informed and efficacious manner. However, the lesson for all is that online technology is at its most effective in parliamentary politics, where the pressures of time are less, resources more abundant and the need is greater. The brilliance of e-democracy is that it can give citizens a route into the political process that is complimentary to representative democracy. However, it will only become another citizen-led protest medium unless elected representatives and institutions get in on the action and think of e-democracy as a collection of techniques and tools rather than a threatening foothold for direct democracy. Only with their committed involvement can the potential of e-democracy be realised for the benefit of democracy.'

Which of the hopes and fears inspired by the prospect of e-democracy have proved realistic to date?

●●

 ## What you should have learnt from reading this chapter

- The focus of political studies in examining Athenian democracy is not the historical events of fifth-century BC Athens in themselves, nor even their causes and consequences. What should be noted, however, are the arguments surrounding the meaning of democracy, its supposed virtues and the criticisms made of it: its direct nature, its values of equality and citizen development, and its potential instability.

- Certain of these remain relevant today, and reflect cleavages of opinion that have existed throughout the modern debate about democracy.

- Historical circumstances are relevant only if they have a bearing upon those arguments, and in terms of the numbers of citizens involved and the economic and social arrangements of Athens they undoubtedly do.

- Andrew Dilnot of the Institute of Fiscal Studies has argued that 'the experience of Greek and Roman citizenship does indeed survive as a memory, and the good we see in it we want for ourselves. But now we are only happy to implement it with guarantees that all will be free, to be heard, and not to be excluded capriciously.'[16]

- The democracy of fifth-century Athens was brought to an end by military defeat, brought about at least in part because of instability among the assembly and rivalry for political leadership.

- The idea of democracy went into abeyance, regarded with suspicion even after its revival. What could not be revived was the economic, social and technological environment in which democracy had operated in Athens; what did re-emerge was the idea of communal self-government, of which Athens was to be a symbol, however tenuously appropriate.

 ## Glossary of key terms

Citizen An adult with full legal rights. In Athens, foreigners and slaves were not citizens. Women had citizens' legal rights, but could not vote.
Direct democracy A system in which the public decides directly what law and taxes are to be imposed upon them, and judges those who carry out their decisions. In Athens, this was done at regular mass meetings.
Oligarchy A system of rule by a small number of leaders, rather than by a single figure or a democracy.
Parliamentary government A system in which members of the government arise from, are accountable to, and gain their powers and funding with the consent of, Parliament.
Philosopher King The term used by Plato to describe those people whose natural gifts of moral and intellectual insight make them the right

leaders of society, but who are neglected by democratic systems. This view that some people are unalterably better at government than others is called Élitism.

Relativism The belief that different societies, lifestyles and ideas are not right or wrong in any absolute or objective way, and that all should therefore be tolerated.

Sortition A method of choosing office-holders, such as magistrates, by chance from the citizens' roll. This meant that office-holders could not claim a right to act under their own initiative in the way that modern politicians do.

Likely examination questions

How much can we learn about the principles of democracy from examining the experience of ancient Athens?

Why has ancient Athens exercised so much attraction to modern political theorists?

'The attractions and the dangers of democracy were as obvious to the ancient Greeks as they are to us today.' Discuss.

Helpful websites

A basic introduction to Athenian institutions can be found on the BBC History website at www.bbc.co.uk/history/ancient/greeks/greekdemocracy_01.shtml, and www.bbc.co.uk/history/ancient/greeks/greekcritics_01.shtml.

More demanding and detailed articles are to be found at Demos Classical Athenian Democracy website: www.stoa.org/projects/demos/home.

Recent attempts to put direct democracy into practice are reported at the following websites:

www.hansardsociety.org.uk/programmes/e-democracy

www.edemocracy.gov.uk/default.htm

Suggestions for further reading

The following accounts set the Athenian system within the context of events of the present day in an appropriate style for politics students:

Paul Cartledge, 'Ancient Greeks and Modern Britons', *History Today*, vol. 44, April 1994.

John Dunn (ed.) *Democracy: the Unfinished Journey* (Oxford University Press, 1992), chapters 1–3, and *Setting the People Free: the Story of Democracy* (Atlantic Books, 2005).

David Held, *Models of Democracy*, 2nd edn (Polity Press, 1996) chapter 1.

This title offers a comparison between ancient Athens and liberal democracy in modern America:

Loren J. Samons, *What's Wrong with Democracy? From Athenian Practice to American Worship* (University of California, 2004).

For those seeking greater emphasis on Athens itself, the following historical accounts offer limited comparisons with modern democracy:

History Today, vol. 44, 1994, contains a series of articles examining democracy, many concentrating upon Athens, notably 'What Democracy Meant' by Josiah Ober (January) and 'Democracy and the Philosophers' by Benjamin Barber (August).

P. J. Rhodes, *Athenian Democracy* (Edinburgh University Press, 2004).

J. Thorley, *Athenian Democracy* (Routledge [Lancaster Pamphlets] 2004).

On the use of the Internet to promote political participation, a recent study comparing experience internationally is:

R. K. Gibson, P. Nixon, and S. Ward, (eds), *Political Parties and the Internet: Net Gain?* (Routledge, 2003).

The following article gives a good round-up of some of the key arguments and some important events in the area of electronic democracy:

Nigel Jackson, 'E-Democracy', *Talking Politics*, April 2003.

The Emergence of Representative Democracy

Contents

Overview

Having dealt with the origins of the idea of democracy, and outlined its relationship with two other related concepts, we need now to consider how democracy as it is familiar to us today came into being as a system of government. This chapter will identify some of the key thinkers involved in recasting the idea of democracy for a modern context, comparing and contrasting their views from the time of the Enlightenment onwards. It will also explore the continuing divisions within the democratic tradition, and the competing arguments of principle for and against them. After you have read this chapter, you should be able to distinguish between these ideas and evaluate them for yourself.

Key issues to be covered in this chapter

- Who were the leading figures credited with 'rediscovering' democracy?
- What are the differences between participatory and representative democracy?
- What were the differences between these conceptions, and that of Athenian democracy?
- How do these conceptions of democracy relate to the main political ideologies?
- What are the strengths and weaknesses of each of these conceptions of democracy?

Historical background

For two millenniums from the ending of Athenian democracy by the Macedonians in 322 BC, the idea of popular sovereignty lay largely dormant among political writers and activists. Those who sought to identify the source of legitimate authority saw it as being found in military prowess, birth, tenure of land, or most often (and sometimes allegedly expressed through the preceding) divine right.

Until the thirteenth century, the very term 'democracy' went into obscurity and, when it emerged in translations of Aristotle, it bore his pejorative slant, as an inherently unjust form of government, involving the oppression of the public by the poorest (if most numerous) faction. Some features of European systems of government, particularly of the Italian city-republics of the thirteenth to eighteenth centuries, involved elective offices, and even public debates and votes, but none on the scale of Athens, and none that would have used the word 'democracy' of themselves. Charles I may have claimed in his answer to the Nineteen Propositions of 1642 that Britain was partly a democracy, but the Levellers and Diggers, free-thinking land reformers of the Civil War era, disagreed. Their campaigns were short lived and enjoyed limited support, and it was not until the late eighteenth century that democracy emerged in anything like the forms we recognise today – and the forms it took, even as an abstract concept, bore little relation to either the practice of Ancient Athens or to the ideological claims imposed by modem writers upon the historical structure of Athenian democracy.

As it emerged in the intellectual tumult of the Enlightenment, democracy formed two distinct traditions, both claiming a classical heritage, and each with its own myriad variants. The distinction between two schools of democracy made here is broad and, in some respects, superficial because it rests upon structure: nonetheless, that structure tells us much about the purpose and justifications of these forms – and points to the strengths and weaknesses of those more abstract conceptions.

Participatory democracy

The growing awareness of, and interest in, classical history in the eighteenth century led some writers and politicians to believe that the principles of Athens could be resuscitated in a similar structure, in which all adult men could directly create laws and hold officials accountable. Best known of these is Jean-Jacques Rousseau (1712–82) whose key work, *The Social Contract* (1762), argued that sovereignty could not be transferred to other persons, and only personal participation in the making of laws could ever allow men to be free.

Like earlier writers, Rousseau argued against systems under the title of democracy, assuming them to involve government by a self-interested majority over a minority, a structure he perceived to be impractical as well as improper. Nonetheless, Rousseau is regarded as a pioneer of modern democratic theory because he believed that the true sovereign authority is to be found among the populace, in the form of what he called the 'General Will'. The **General Will** is the term used to describe the opinion formed by a citizenry together after public discussion, and is characterised by two features:

1. It is as close to unanimity as possible (although Rousseau makes it explicit that dissent does not invalidate the General Will);
2. It is arrived at by citizens' consideration not of their private, individual interests and opinions, but of the interests of the community of which they are a part.

Thus, a majority decision – even a unanimous one – may not reflect the General Will, but rather the 'sum of private wills' or 'the will of all': the combination of a series of private, short-term decisions by voters neglecting their more important civic identity and interests. The sort of 'pocket-book' voting condemned by critics of the Conservatives, in constituencies such as Basildon in Essex in the 1992 general election, might be a modern example of this, and those critics might point, too, to the apparent unwillingness of those Conservative voters to express those 'selfish' interests in opinion polls prior to (and even immediately upon emerging from) casting their votes. At the 2005 general election, specific appeals to sectional interests were as evident as ever: from the Liberal Democrats to students over tuition fees, especially in university seats such as Cardiff Central; from the Conservatives to higher earners who might benefit from reduced direct taxation, especially in suburban seats where they were competing with the Liberal Democrats who proposed more progressive taxation; and from Labour to so-called 'school-gate mums' who were thought to have interests in provision of childcare, education expenditure and the government's tax credits scheme.

The General Will, by contrast, emerges, Rousseau suggests, at best spontaneously from a public discussion and vote under the right social and political conditions. These include the prohibition of sectional associations or parties, an austere and egalitarian economy, and a community small enough for all citizens to be able to recognise one another. Since these conditions have never prevailed, it is difficult for us to imagine whether the General Will exists at all, or what it might declare if it did: David Thomson has compared this with the refusal of the British public – at great risk and cost to themselves privately – to conciliate with the Nazis in the darkest days of Dunkirk and the Battle of Britain;[1] a similar spirit might be identified with public resistance to threats to the community from terrorism by Irish Republicans in the 1970s and 1980s, and most recently from those responsible for the bombings in London in July 2005.

Examples such as this highlight the essential problem of the General Will, however, namely that it can be distinguished from the Will of All only by reference to the subjective and unprovable moral quality of motive, or goodwill. Hypocrisy, as the saying goes, is the compliment vice pays to virtue. The very same decision could be motivated by private or public interest and, likewise, two contrary opinions could both conceivably arise from sincere consideration of community interest. It even remains possible that the General Will could on occasion reside in the minority. Rousseau did bequeath to modern political thought one central notion, however: that the direct participation of the public could free us from the tensions and competition, the anxieties and privations of atomised, isolated society by allowing us to rediscover our communal identity. This was a belief that was to underpin leftist analysis of democracy for the next two centuries.

Rousseau's analysis first saw expression (or abuse) in the events of the French Revolution from 1789 onwards. The authors of the Declaration of the Rights of Man borrowed the passion and the lexicon, if not the ideas, of Rousseau in arguing that authority did not proceed from the divine right of Louis XVI to rule France, but that 'the principle of all sovereignty emanates essentially from the nation. No group of men, no individual, can exercise any authority which does not specifically emanate from it,' and, even more explicitly, 'The law is the expression of the general will. All citizens have the right to take part personally, or through their representatives, in the making of the law.'

The revolution proved a disappointment to idealists: universal male suffrage was not granted, civil liberties were suspended for political associations and trade unions, and France descended into factionalism and bloodshed, from which the military dictatorship of Napoleon emerged. In fact, it is widely acknowledged that Rousseau's ideas, though perhaps an early inspiration for some, were more of a symbol than a blueprint for those who ran the Republic. Though streets were named after him, and statues of him were erected, he was read by few and followed by fewer of the revolution's disciples. Nonetheless, his central notion of popular, often spontaneous, and even violent action and opinion as the legitimate source of authority was thrown into sharp relief by the revolution: it excited radicals, worried liberals, and horrified conservatives.

The reactions to the French Revolution reflect assessments of democracy still valid today. To its advocates, such as Wordsworth, popular participation was a source of energy, unity of purpose and moral authority; to liberals, unrestrained participation had destroyed individual rights which they held to be the purpose of government – even Thomas Paine had been imprisoned for dissent; conservatives, such as Edmund Burke, shuddered at the sight of ancient and stable institutions, such as the monarchy, nobility and the church, being razed to the ground and (still more importantly) the dismissal of all of society's established conventions and values (those that Burke called 'prejudices') in favour of the new and mechanically rationalist democratic ideal. Conservatism regarded itself as that which G. K. Chesterton was to call 'a democracy of the dead', in which the opinions and ideas of those no longer alive (or, indeed, yet to be born) are treated with the respect due to them.

It was in his analysis of the French Revolution, *The Origins of Totalitarian Democracy* (1952), that J. L. Talmon attacked the notion of a general will as the myth to which a sequence of revolutionary gangs, each more brutal than the last, laid claim. 'In marrying this concept with the principle of popular sovereignty, the popular self-expression,' Talmon wrote, 'Rousseau gave rise to totalitarian democracy . . . . There is such a thing as an objective general will, whether willed or not willed by anybody. To become a reality, it must be willed by the people. If the people does not will it, it must be made to will it, for the general will is latent in the people's will.'[2] Thus the moral and practical limitations identified in democracy in Athens reappeared in different form in the modern world.

Communitarianism: can the General Will be found in the modern world?

Various attempts have been made to ease participation by bringing decision-making down to a more local level, involving a specific area or group of people small enough to allow direct contribution by individuals.

Such aims have found expression in kibbutzim and in the tradition of town meetings in the United States, as well as in various communes and colonies founded in America and Europe since the 1960s, though many have failed, either through internal weaknesses or external pressures. They were also the foundation underlying inner-city protest organisations and committees in America in the 1960s, and the community development projects established in Birmingham, London and Newcastle in the 1970s. Other projects have defined themselves by race, religion or gender to establish women's groups, or organisations such as the Black Panthers and Black Muslims in the United States. Characteristically, each of these has tried to recover to a marginalised or disempowered quarter of society some control over its own destiny, shared equally among its members. More recently, these ideas have played a part in the establishment of local neighbourhood offices in many urban local authorities, and resurfaced with the development of 'Communitarianism' by Amitai Etzioni in the 1990s. **Communitarianism** is widely believed to have influenced the social and political reform programme of the Labour government since 1997 and, for that reason alone, deserves particular attention.

In a series of publications, notably *The Spirit of Community* (1993), Etzioni argued that small communities of people could find and express common values constituting an objective sense of the good which would strengthen their communities and improve the quality of their daily lives by making them more supportive to one another.[3] This contrasts sharply with the liberal notions of relativism, privacy and diversity in moral issues. In *The Monochrome Society* (2001)[4] and *The Common Good* (2004),[5] Etzioni went on to assert the idea of objective social values against libertarian forces and in the context of global telecommunications and international terrorism. As law and order rose up the political agenda in Britain, Communitarian ideas caught the eye of Labour leaders as a means of being 'tough on crime' without appearing simply authoritarian as the Conservatives were accused of being, but by giving voice to communal aspirations for order, decency and respect. Geoff Mulgan, founder of the pro-Communitarian think-tank, Demos, became an adviser to Tony Blair and, though Etzioni himself was rarely credited, ideas of the community and civil society as the basis of social values resonated through the speeches of Blair and the writing of the chief academic architect of the Third Way, Anthony Giddens:

> Our relationships with and commitments to others are not add-ons to our personalities: they make us who we are. Notions of mutuality and interdependence are not abstract ideals: they are facts of life.[6]

> We all depend on collective goods for our independence; and all our lives are enriched – or impoverished – by the communities to which we belong. A key challenge of progressive politics is to use the state as an enabling force, protecting effective communities and voluntary organizations and encouraging their growth to tackle new needs.[7]

> The theme of community is fundamental to the new politics, but not just as an abstract slogan . . . 'Community' doesn't imply trying to capture lost forms of social solidarity; it refers to practical means of furthering the social and material refurbishment of neighbourhoods, towns and larger local areas.[8]

Under Labour in government, this has meant granting communities freedom to establish new schools or determine their organisation; to initiate the imposition of Anti-Social Behaviour Orders; and initiating a campaign for a stronger sense of citizenship to be inculcated in schools and shown by those applying for British nationality In 2000, experienced Labour candidate and Fabian writer, Paul Richards, called for the party to reinvent itself as a 'communitarian party'.[9] For Prime Minister Blair and Home Secretary Jack Straw, these values were explicitly underpinned by their Christian Socialism but, by 2003, more secular Home Secretary David Blunkett was applauding 'a surge of interest amongst political theorists in civic republican thinking, often associated with communitarian philosophers' having argued that 'ancient Greece has much to teach us'.[10] Simon Davies of civil liberties pressure group, Privacy International, told the *Guardian* in 2004 that 'if you look at Labour's policy documents and legislation, it [*sic*] is riddled with concepts of "the common good" which take their cue from Etzioni's philosophy',[11] and Tony Blair's 2005 victory speech on the steps of Number 10 Downing Street made a sombre appeal for the restoration of respect as a value in British society.

Practical projects in this line have often involved hundreds of people in direct decision-making about matters of their own transport, housing, education, health and welfare, and taxation. The Home Office claims that 16 million people in Britain are involved in some sort of civic voluntary work. They rely, however, upon the right circumstances and properly tailored objectives to achieve success. Saul Alinsky, the American writer whose practical work in this field was an inspiration to others in Britain as well, found that community politics worked well only when led by a (professional) organiser, usually imported from outside. There was also a tendency for apathy to creep in once the initial cause of the group's formation (a rent strike, the blocking of a new road, or the protection of a school from closure, for example) had been resolved. The experience of community schemes has been that, like industrial co-operatives, they have little control over the general policy context in which they operate, 'totally incapable of altering the logic of delivery of services' as one commentator has put it. They may even become reliant upon subsidy from local authorities above them, and thus be drawn into the liberal democratic network to which they were intended to supply an alternative but to which Alinsky saw community democracy as essentially complementary. In the increasingly globally interdependent world of modern economics and communication, this danger of unrealistic isolationism becomes even greater.[12]

Worse still, community politics suffers from the same potential weaknesses as all other democratic schemes, including the danger of the tyranny of the majority. Many observers were concerned when, in 1993, the possibility arose of the Isle of Dogs Neighbourhood Office budget falling into the hands of the racist British National Party after they won one of the ward's three seats at a by-election.

Though that outcome was avoided, the BNP has, since 2002, won over a dozen seats in towns and cities throughout the North and Midlands, including eight in Burnley alone. Etzioni's Communitarianism has even been compared to Fascism on the grounds that it ushers in the smothering rule of 'shared moral values' without placing constraints upon the scope of those values: what, for instance, if the shared morals of a community (and they surely cannot all be universally shared) dictate that there shall be no sale of alcohol, or no publication of obscene material, or no toleration of victims of AIDS, or of those accused of any of these or more, even though this restricts a minority. The unruly demonstrations on the Paulsgrove estate in Portsmouth in 2000, and some subsequent assaults on alleged paedophiles (including an attack upon the home of a paediatrician in South Wales by local self-styled vigilantes) are an illustration of how widely held passionate views can manifest themselves if not contained by the political process. Etzioni has insisted that beliefs such as these are not shared morals, but 'over-reactions', and are unlikely to spring from communities which 'draw on interpersonal bonds to encourage members to abide by shared values, such as "Do not throw your rubbish out of the window" and "Mind the children when you drive".' Etzioni might point out that the hatreds involved are often stirred by powerful, corporate forces not controlled by the community, and which Communitarianism might itself contain – notably the media. One can almost hear J. L. Talmon asking why, however, if Etzioni already knows – like the French revolutionaries – what the General Will intends, he need ask the community at all. He states specifically that 'communities should be governed by constitutional democracies and not simply majority rule'. Yet, in contrasting the alienation, breakdown and 'moral anarchy' he sees in modern liberal democracies with the supposed consensual shared values of local communities, Etzioni presumes that something like a General Will exists, more compelling than a mere majority, and that communities sharing the same territory will not espouse contrary moral values. Surely it is precisely the fact that this is true that has brought us to the state of affairs of which he laments? It seems that Rousseauvian idealistic yearning for civic virtue has survived Schumpeter and Fukuyama undaunted. Etzioni claims that 'Communitarian thinking's roots spring from ancient Greece': its dilemmas are just as old.[13]

Box 3.1 Three participatory democrats

Jean-Jacques Rousseau (1712–78) was a citizen of Geneva, a small city-state of the sort he believed capable of reclaiming the inheritance of Athens. Rousseau believed that humankind is corrupted by society, and that we are made greedy, hostile and shallow by the competition for private property, status and power. He argued that an ideal society would be run along Athenian lines, but with fewer inequalities of wealth, and that, in discussion among citizens, a 'General Will' would emerge that reflected the collective interests of the community. Though he died shortly before the French Revolution, he became an important figurehead for its leaders, who claimed to be following his principles.

Charles Fourier (1772–1837) was associated with practical attempts to establish communes (he called them 'phalanxes') along collective, democratic lines. Workers were to be allowed to change jobs as regularly as they liked; children would learn only what they wanted; and childcare and housework would be collectively organised to liberate women. Although a number of such communities was established in France and America (some by Robert Owen), none lasted long: apart from his naivety about human nature, Fourier himself relied upon funding from wealthy aristocrats, and was deeply anti-industrial, hoping to restore a craft-based society against the rising tide of the Industrial Revolution.

Karl Marx (1818–83), on the other hand, appreciated and even admired the productive capacity of industrial capitalism. He argued that democracy would come about only after the working class took ownership of the means of production and the social control which went with it, through education, the media and religion. This would be a potentially violent and ultimately worldwide struggle, in which Marx himself participated by the establishment of the First International Working Men's Association in London in 1864. Marx believed that, once private ownership had been eliminated, political dispute would almost entirely disappear, as it reflected class conflict, and only administrative questions would remain to be resolved by localised participatory democracy.

Socialist visions of democracy

In the nineteenth century, once the turbulence of the Napoleonic Wars was over, **participatory democracy** became the claim of, at various times, co-operatives, anarchists and Marxists. The common feature of these democratic schemes was the attention they gave to the question of property. The co-operative movement, pioneered by figures such as Charles Fourier and Robert Owen (1771–1858), called for the reconstruction of society upon a 'socially responsible' basis: the surplus output of new agricultural and industrial means of production would be reinvested in the community which had created it, because property would be held in common, and services, such as education and childcare, health and housing, would be provided equally and freely to all. All the schemes designed or established by such Utopian Socialists presumed or promised an element of self-government, through the factory or village community, or through a co-operative or trade union structure. This might be through direct participation in meetings, ballots, or consultation. Three distinctive features of the view of democracy involved here emerge which are common to leftist conceptions, and have their roots in Rousseau:

1. Since we acquire our character and values not through individual rational thought but from our environment, democracy consists not of the expression of those externally imposed values and opinions but of the liberation of our true potential from the competitive society in which it is currently imprisoned. This search for this General Will, or Marx's 'Species Being', necessarily requires the appropriate context.
2. That context is for all leftist writers largely economic and partly cultural. The existence of private property and the expropriation of profit from labourers were seen as inimical to democracy by Marxists and Utopians alike. While the basic values of society are competitive, and reinforced by the wealth of capitalists, democracy is meaningless. Common ownership and education supportive of co-operative values would foster a wholly different set of interests and ideas around which truly democratic decision-making would revolve.
3. Such decision-making, it is anticipated by most socialist writers, would be mostly administrative in nature, in contrast to the politics of competing interests which dominate our system. With property removed as a source of conflict, disputes would be, as Rousseau envisaged, about the best means of investing and distributing

resources in the communal interest, rather than about which private interest has most right to those resources. Marx and Engels envisaged the eventual 'withering away' of the state so that democracy would operate at a much more local and direct level; and they acknowledged that this was an expectation shared by Utopian Socialists: 'The French have recently interpreted this as meaning that in a true democracy the political state is annihilated.'

This situation of 'the end of politics' is the one towards which Stalinist and other Communist-led one-party states claimed to be working in the twentieth century. In place of a bourgeois democracy, dismissed by Marx as 'deciding once in three or six years which member of the ruling class is to misrepresent the people in parliament', Soviet democracy offered direct participation through the party (which included 10 per cent of the adult population), in the factory or farm, granting control over the means of production, and genuine social equality and growing prosperity as the key conditions of liberation and democracy. Once decisions were made, they would be rigorously enforced without further equivocation, according to the doctrine of democratic **centralism**.

What, they might have asked, is the value of a democracy in which voters choose periodically between indistinguishable candidates who can present themselves to the electorate only because they have the endorsement of the media, conform to established social values, and are backed by huge personal or corporate wealth, with all that that implies? At the time of writing, for example, presidential hopeful George Bush Jr had spent $32 million before even securing the nomination of the Republican Party for the 2000 American election. The real formation of policy in capitalism, this case argues, goes on elsewhere, and elections are a meaningless charade. Thus, Rousseau stated that the English were free only at election times, and that the use they made of that freedom forfeited any claim to any more; Tanzanian socialist leader Julius Nyerere, asked by an American visitor how he justified a one-party state, replied that America has one too, but – characteristic of the nation's extravagance – it had two parties! This was the essence of Lenin's belief that Western democracy is 'curtailed, poor, false; a democracy only for the rich, for the minority'.

Naturally, this conception of democracy has been the subject of much criticism throughout its development and decline. Most Western politicians and thinkers have dismissed its claim to democratic credentials as laughable, distinguished totalitarianism as quite distinct from democracy, or a 'detour', or else a very distinct, and less agreeable, sort of democracy than the 'genuine' sort. Professor Neil Harding recently concluded that 'it is almost universally conceded that one of the principal factors leading to the discrediting of Communism was its neglect of meaningful democracy'. Most writers, such as S. E. Finer in his classic study *Comparative Government* (1970), rightly identified the key distinction between Soviet-style and liberal democracies as one of our view of identity (whether there is such a phenomenon as a collective or civic identity) and interests – whether they can be ascertained 'scientifically' and objectively, or whether they are the subject of dispute to be resolved in terms of his or her own judgement. Finer attacked the Soviet model as 'this peculiar view', and derided the notion that 'The party, therefore basing itself upon the scientific principles of Marxism-Leninism, always expresses what the majority want, even when majority opinion as actually and fiercely expressed is flatly opposed to what the party proposes to do'.[14] Francis Fukuyama argued in 'The End of History' (*The National Interest*, 1989) that this bogus democracy had been defeated in historical struggle by the liberal sort more familiar to us. It is to this type that we now turn.

Representative democracy

The version of democracy which emerged in the eighteenth century and which came to be the most commonplace form in the modern Western world is known as representative democracy. As its name implies, it is characterised by the sovereignty, not of the population directly, but of others representing them. Representative democracy, also commonly linked to liberal democracy, has three key features:

1. Regular elections in which citizens do not control policy directly themselves, but rather select representatives – MPs or senators, for example – to undertake that work on their behalf. The sheer

Box 3.2 Examples of classical, direct and representative democracy

	Classical	Direct	Representative
Population	250,000	6,800,000	60,000,000
Electorate	40,000 citizens: free Athenian males over twenty.	All adult nationals.	All adult nationals.
Legislature	Assembly: composed of all citizens, at least 6,000 of whom had to attend before business could begin.	Law-making divided between national diet, twenty-three cantons and local public meetings.	Ultimate sovereignty rests with Commons of 646 elected MPs.
Frequency of voting	Assembly met forty times a year, often for days at a time.	National referendums on average nine times a year; local referendums and meetings more often.	Commons and local councils elected every four to five years.
Executive	Officials chosen mostly by sortition, often restricted to citizens over thirty. Terms varied from a day to a year.	At canton level and below, officials questioned and elected at public meetings.	Cabinet appointed by monarch from main group(s) in Commons.
Social context	Pre-industrial slave society with great inequality; military important.	Prosperous, ethnically divided society.	Large, stable, increasing pluralism; economic decline.

Classical features based upon Athenian system, 5th century BC; direct democracy on Swiss Confederation of Cantons; representative democracy on United Kingdom Constitution.

numbers of citizens in modern democracies makes the practice of direct democracy effectively impossible in most contexts. The Swiss system of cantons (see Box 3.2) is a rare exception.

2. Limits are imposed upon what the majority of such representatives may do – usually by means of a constitution (as in the United States), or set of conventions, or by separating law-making powers between different institutions such as branches (legislature, executive and judiciary) or levels (national and regional) of government. This limitation of state action is the reason such systems are characterised as **'protective' democracy**, because the democracy involved is intended for the purpose of protecting individual rights.

3. Also reflecting the liberal tradition is the commitment to political liberties for all citizens, such as freedom of speech, freedom to form parties or associations, and the freedom to stand in elections and thus grant electors a choice of representative. These rights may be set out in some entrenched legal document such as a permanent bill of rights.

Early advocates of this theory, such as American revolutionary and later president, James Madison, were keen students of classical history, and (as the architecture of the new United States capital in Washington emphasised), revered the ideas of Roman law and Greek participation. Yet many of the Founding Fathers agreed with Governor Elbridge Gerry that 'the evils we experience flow from the excess of democracy'. Indeed, for most of representative democracy's history, its advocates would have shuddered at the second half of its title. Why, then did they – and do they still – accept what looks like a half-baked democracy?

We have already seen the arguments advanced by Edmund Burke about the nature and limits of representation, but a more comprehensive defence of that view was made around the same time by Madison. As an active revolutionary in the campaign to liberate America from the arbitrary rule of George III, Madison rejected tyranny based upon the whims of remote individuals, and recognised that only government accountable to wider opinion could ever be regarded as just. It was the protection of the rights of individuals, however, rather than the expression of public, even majority, opinion that was of greatest priority to the Founding Fathers, even in their public pronouncements (their personal motives are an historical question). Democracy was a useful tool, but no more than that. Madison and others outlined a case for restricted democratic structures in editions of *The Federalist Papers* during 1787–8 which reflects the logic of representative, rather than participatory, democracy in concise form.

Believers in representative democracy begin from the presumption that politics is inevitably about the resolution of conflicts between competing interests or, as Madison called them, 'factions', and that attempts to pretend otherwise are mistaken. The notion of a General Will, or sense of overriding civic duty is a shibboleth, and a dangerous one because, if elevated to the power which such a force would merit, the opinion claiming that title will be no more than a tyranny.

If the sort of consensus about social values necessary for direct democracy to work ever existed, it could only be in a small community. (Rousseau said that his system could work only in a citizenry small enough for everyone to know everyone else) and one with such a close-knit identity as to stifle diversity and discussion. Otherwise, it would require a culture of toleration and submission to the rule of the majority developed over a very long period in a stable society.

'So strong is the propensity of mankind to fall into mutual animosities', wrote Madison, 'that when no substantial occasion presents itself, the most frivolous and fanciful distinctions have been sufficient to kindle their unfriendly passions and excite their most violent conflicts.' Oligarchies and dictatorships tend to resolve these conflicts exclusively in the interests of those in power at the expense of the basic liberties of those excluded from it; democracy tends to keep the government in check. Yet even democracy can be oppressive, if it allows a majority faction to invade the basic rights of a minority, say in matters of religion, or, as Madison anticipated was most likely, property ownership.

This 'tyranny of the majority' became a preoccupation of nineteenth-century liberals and conservatives such as de Tocqueville and, to forestall it, representative democracy places a series of barriers between transitory popular opinion and power. In America these took the form of Congress, which Madison hoped would be filled with 'fit characters' who, having survived the scrutiny of election, would be best suited to 'refine' public opinion, and 'discern the interest of their country'. Moreover, having borrowed his notions of human nature from Hobbes and of representation from Burke, Madison reflected in the limits of state structure and power the ideas of Montesquieu and Locke. The danger of factional exploitation is further resisted in most liberal democracies by the separation of power and the establishment of local authorities with specific duties distinct from those of the national assembly. Around the fragmented state, liberal democracy encourages a plurality of interest and pressure groups that provides further points of access to the political system. This **pluralist** scenario was admiringly depicted by Robert Dahl in his *Who Governs? Democracy and Power in an American City* (1961).[15]

Box 3.3 Three liberal democrats

Lawyer **James Madison** (1751–1836) was the secretary of the convention that wrote the American Constitution in 1787, and became the fourth American President in 1809. In *The Federalist Papers*, he argued for representative government limited by the separation of powers, and a bill of rights to contain the volatile, short-sighted and potentially violent propensities of the public and the factions into which they would split in a pure democracy.

John Stuart Mill (1806–73) was the son of Utilitarian philosopher, James Mill, who raised him at home to give him an unusually intense education. Mill believed in individual liberty and greater democracy, including the vote for women which, as an MP, he proposed in the 1860s. Mill, however, did not believe that the vote was a natural right, and argued that it should be denied to paupers and illiterates, that the educated should have more than one vote, and that voting should be public.

Robert Dahl (1915–), a professor at Yale University, is one of the best known of the American political scientists who emerged after World War II to try to recast ideas of democracy to show that liberal democracy was its best realisable interpretation. Dahl made these arguments in principle in *A Preface to Democratic Theory* and, in *Who Governs?*, he asserted that the exemplary American city of New Haven was run by a system of pluralist democracy, which came to be called 'Polyarchy', or the distribution of power among many competing groups, thus offering multiple access points to decision-making for the public.

All of this was, as David Held has recognised, 'a far cry from the classical ideals of civic life and the public realm',[16] and modern democrats are even less impressed when we add to this description a voting public in most liberal democracies before the twentieth century often smaller as a proportion of adults than that of Athens. Madison certainly did not conceive of blacks, women or the unpropertied as forming part of the public opinion which caused him such anxiety. Yet it was as the barriers towards those citizens' participation fell that the advocates of the representative model restricted their aims still further.

Throughout the nineteenth and early twentieth centuries, liberal democracies such as Britain and America gradually granted the vote to a larger and larger proportion of the public, taking down barriers of religion, race, class and eventually sex. This was all done, however, within the broad conceptual presumptions of representative, parliamentary democracy, and the vote was rarely, if ever, regarded as a right in any absolute sense. Perhaps the keenest advocate of his time of the extension of the franchise, John Stuart Mill, argued in *Considerations on Representative Government* (1861) that voting is 'strictly a matter of duty . . . the voter is under an absolute moral obligation to consider the interest of the public, not his private advantage', and not sharing Rousseauvian hopes of any General Will emerging, nor ideas of equality, Mill argued for open voting, and the restriction of the franchise to those passing basic tests of reading and writing, while the more able were rewarded with multiple votes. 'No one but a fool' wrote Mill, 'and a fool of a peculiar description, feels offended by the acknowledgement that there are others whose opinion, and even whose wish, is entitled to a greater amount of consideration than his . . . It is not useful, but hurtful, that the constitution of the country should declare ignorance to be entitled to as much political power as knowledge'. Thus democracy was justified in terms of its improvement of public policy, and indeed of the citizenry itself, but this placed considerable constraints upon the extent and effect of that democracy. 'The idea of rational democracy is not that the people themselves govern, but that they have security for good government' Mill concluded: 'The best government must be the government of the wisest, and these must always be few.'

Not surprisingly, this view has come in for a good deal of critical review, and was wryly described by Graeme Duncan as 'democratic

Platonism'[17] for its seeming attempt to tie together a recognition of human inequality with an attempt at popular control over government. But it was in the twentieth century that representative democracy tailored its aspirations even more trimly than before. As populations, and the proportions of those populations entitled to vote, grew, and the technology of transport, communication and production rendered society more and more impersonal and collectivised, writers began to question the reasonable prospects for mass participation in politics, and the theory of Competitive Élitism was born.

Competitive Élitism is most closely associated with Max Weber (1864–1920) and Joseph Schumpeter (1883–1946), and is both a descriptive and a normative theory – that is to say that Weber and Schumpeter believed that Western democracies were not democratic in any participatory sense because any attempt to render them so would end in disaster. Weber concluded that the demands placed upon governments, and the advance of technical expertise, have led to a technocratic regime in most modern advanced industrial states, in which increasingly specialist, self-confident and institutionalised expert bureaucratic structures form a 'steel-hard cage' within which democratic discussion must take place. Schumpeter was still more pessimistic about the prospects of democracy: though, as an economist, he regarded himself as a socialist, this was a greater reflection of his faith in planning than in equality. He believed that, in modern society, politics is necessarily conducted through a hierarchy of institutions and people: detailed decisions are made by bureaucrats; the general thrust of policy is guided by political leaders, informed by elected, professional politicians; the great mass of people, said Schumpeter in another use of the animal analogy of which élitists are so fond, for reasons of either intellect or resources, 'is incapable of action other than a stampede'. Schumpeter saw politics as analogous to business, with voters no more capable of controlling policy than apathetic, advertising-led consumers are capable of researching and redesigning complex products. Rather, we choose between competing leaderships and parties just as we select insurance firms or soap powder on the basis of our best knowledge and instinct.

This approach echoed the work of Robert Michels (1876–1936), a student of Weber's, which found that the internal mechanisms of political parties are subject to an '**Iron Law of Oligarchy**', whereby a small number of leading figures inevitably controls organisations. As a result, 'democracy does not mean and cannot mean that the people actually rule in any obvious sense of the terms "people" and "rule". Democracy means only that the people have the opportunity of accepting or refusing the men who are to rule them.' Any attempt or pretence to involve large numbers of citizens more widely in political decision-making would be either laughably impractical, or – more likely – dangerously vulnerable to manipulation, as the 'mass movements' of Soviet Communism and Nazism (from which he had fled) had been.

Box 3.4 Three Élitists

Max Weber (1864–1920) has been described as 'a liberal in despair': principally a sociologist, he did not write at length about what should be the arrangements of the political system, but concentrated on what does happen in practice, and what it implies about the limits on what liberty and participation are achievable in modern society. Both a professor and a politician, Weber came to the conclusion that the increasing size and complexity of public organisations meant that the roles of the bureaucracy and of 'legal-rational' rather than 'charismatic' authority were bound to increase. This meant that democracy would necessarily be limited to the choice by the public of professional politicians who would help to guide these organisations.

The work of **Robert Michels** (1876–1936), a student of Weber's, focused upon the limitations of the internal democracy of the institutions through which public opinion could be conveyed. Because of differing levels of resources and commitment, and the inevitable competition for control, all large organizations, such as pressure groups and political parties, are ultimately run by an élite according to the 'iron law of oligarchy', and so cannot be regarded as authentically democratic vehicles.

Joseph Schumpeter (1883–1950) drew some corresponding conclusions from his examination of public aptitude and interest in politics in *Capitalism, Socialism and Democracy* in 1942. Having left the Europe of the dictators for America, Schumpeter argued that the most impact the public could hope for on public policy was the opportunity to vote for politicians who would work with administrators and technocrats to guide the direction of government. Public participation at a more detailed level would, he suggested, be at best ill-informed, and at worst open to manipulation.

Competitive Élitism reflects perhaps more strongly than any fore-going theory of representative democracy the perilous dangers of pursuing the 'holy grail' of the General Will. Competitive Élitism also comes in for the most severe criticism of all forms of representative democracy. Held concludes that Schumpeter's attitude to the general public 'places considerable strain on the claim of "competitive elitism" to be democratic . . . Along with Max Weber, Schumpeter too hastily closed the exploration of other possible models in democratic theory and practice.' Lastly, then we must consider whether there are any options other than pious hope or pessimism in the search for democracy today.

Box 3.5 Different views on participation

Source A: Rousseau, The Social Contract, *1762*
'As soon as public service ceases to be the chief business of the citizens and they would rather serve with their money than their persons, the State is not far from its fall. When it is necessary to march out to war, they pay troops and stay at home: when it is necessary to meet in council, they name deputies and stay at home. By reason of idleness and money, they end by having soldiers to enslave their country and representatives to sell it . . . Sovereignty, for the same reason as makes it inalienable, cannot be represented; it lies essentially in the general will, and will does not admit of representation . . . The people of England regards itself as free; but it is grossly mistaken; it is free only during the election of members of parliament. As soon as they are elected, slavery overtakes it, and it is nothing. The use it makes of the short moments of liberty it enjoys shows indeed that it deserves to lose them.'

Source B: J. S. Mill, Considerations on Representative Government, *1866*
'It has been seen, that the dangers incident to a representative democracy are of two kinds: danger of a low grade of intelligence in the representative body, and in the popular opinion which controls it; and danger of class legislation on the part of the numerical majority, these being all composed of the same class. We have next to consider, how far it is possible so to organize the democracy, as, without interfering materially with the characteristic benefits of democratic government, to do away with these two great evils, or at least to abate them, in the utmost degree attainable by human contrivance.'

Source C: Joseph Schumpeter, Capitalism, Socialism and Democracy, 1936
'Party and machine politicians are simply the response to the fact that the electoral mass is incapable of action other than a stampede, and they constitute an attempt to regulate political competition exactly similar to the corresponding practices of a trade association. The psycho-technics of party management and party advertising, slogans and marching tunes, are not accessories. They are of the essence of politics.'

Source D: The Communitarian Network platform statement, 2005 (first issued 1991)
'Not Majoritarian But Strongly Democratic
'Communitarians are not majoritarians. The success of the democratic experiment in ordered liberty (rather than unlimited license) depends, not on fiat or force, but on building shared values, habits and practices that assure respect for one another's rights and regular fulfillment of personal, civic, and collective responsibilities. Successful policies are accepted because they are recognized to be legitimate, rather than imposed. We say to those who would impose civic or moral virtues by suppressing dissent (in the name of religion, patriotism, or any other cause), or censoring books, that their cure is ineffective, harmful, and morally untenable. At the same time divergent moral positions need not lead to cacophony. Out of genuine dialogue clear voices can arise, and shared aspirations can be identified and advanced.

'Communitarians favour strong democracy. That is, we seek to make government more representative, more participatory, and more responsive to all members of the community. We seek to find ways to accord citizens more information, and more say, more often. We seek to curb the role of private money, special interests, and corruption in government. Similarly, we ask how 'private governments,' whether corporations, labour unions, or voluntary associations, can become more responsive to their members and to the needs of the community.

'Communitarians do not exalt the group as such, nor do they hold that any·set of group values is *ipso facto* good merely because such values originate in a community. Indeed, some communities (say, neo-Nazis) may foster reprehensible values. Moreover, communities that glorify their own members by vilifying those who do not belong are at best imperfect. Communitarians recognize – indeed, insist – that communal values must be judged by external and overriding criteria, based on shared human experience.'

Source E: Nick Cohen, 'When self-help is not enough', New Statesman, 3 April 2000. Cohen is reporting on a communitarian project to improve Balsall Heath, a deprived area of Birmingham.

'Balsall Heath and the new cheerleaders of modernity were united in the person of Dick Atkinson, a sociologist at Birmingham University who has worked in the city's slums for 30 years. Atkinson provided Demos with one of its earliest pamphlets – *The Common Sense of Community* – a communitarian tract published in 1995 that rationalized the worries and initiatives of his neighbours. A kind of theory struggled from his musings, which inspired, or at least justified, the emerging postures of old Conservatives and 'new' Labour . . . When he began work in Balsall Heath 30 years ago, he tells me, there was one voluntary agency. There are now 70 busying themselves in what he calls, somewhat euphemistically, "Balsall Heath village" . . . Soon, he will host a conference in Birmingham, "Urban Renaissance", at which delegates will be instructed to learn from the Balsall Heath example. The rather grandiose title isn't complete bluster. The tarts have been driven from the streets by the vigilantes he encouraged – and crime has fallen as a result. Ideas he helped promulgate – zero tolerance and the fostering of self-reliant schools freed from bureaucrats – are now so commonplace that they barely raise an eyebrow.

'The most striking manifestation of autonomy was the direct action against prostitutes . . . The residents organized pickets, disrupted the sex business and noted down the numbers of crawlers . . . No one who knew what Balsall Heath was like can crush all feelings of sympathy for the vigilantes. But there was a touch of the reactionary voyeur about the ecstatic journalists who came up from Fleet Street to praise, in the words of Melanie Phillips, a community which was fighting "those who believe that all values are relative and no one should judge anyone else". Most didn't want to know about the messier side of communitarianism . . . A woman's home was fire-bombed on one occasion, and had bricks, crossbow darts and fireworks arrive though her letterbox and windows at other times . . . But the pimps have not been stopped. Predictably, they have moved to neighbouring Edgbaston, which is becoming so popular with kerb crawlers that its MP is demanding emergency legislation. A practical alternative would be legal, inspected brothels away from homes, but that would be unthinkably relativist.'

In what ways do these writers agree or disagree about the way in which democratic government should be organised?

And the winner is . . .?

Opening a Council of Europe seminar on disillusionment with democracy more than ten years ago, Professor Kenneth Newton of Essex University found that, in the two decades following 1973, nearly 7,500 different books had been published in English with the words 'Democracy' and 'Crisis' in the titles. Among the better known is that of C. B. Macpherson who explained the title of his *The Life and Times of Liberal Democracy* (1977) thus:

> Is liberal democracy, then, to be considered so nearly finished that one may presume now to sketch its life and times? The short answer, prejudging the case I shall be putting, is: 'Yes', if liberal democracy is taken to mean, as it still very generally is, the democracy of a capitalist market society.

Macpherson argued that, if liberal democracy were to survive at all, it would be only by significant changes in property distribution, and at the same time a substantial injection of direct participation by citizens in decision-making through parties, factories or localities. More recently, Adam Lively has urged that 'In the future, we need to escape from the idea that democracy should consist merely of a game of electoral roulette once every five years. We need to think instead of the different levels of democratic control and accountability and representation that different areas of human activity demand.'[18]

Such commentators point to the decreasing respect in which parliamentary institutions are held, and the increasing ungovernability of liberal democracies, in which the law is challenged, sometimes even by riot or terrorist violence, on a more and more regular basis and with growing confidence. In Britain, this has involved everything from illegal protests by environmental groups or refusal to pay the Poll Tax, to the armed struggles of the Provisional IRA or of Al-Qaeda. This, it is claimed, is the result of a political structure that has merely the form of a limited democracy, but embodies none of its values or spirit, and ignores the unequal distribution of power (and therefore access to democracy) between classes, sexes, regions and a host of other social cleavages.

The pessimistic (at least from the point of view of the *status quo*) orthodoxy of the 1970s was replaced in the late 1980s by Fukuyama's triumphant claim that liberal democracy, far from collapsing under the weight of its own hypocrisy, had seen off all comers, and shown itself to be coherent both with itself and with human nature. Since then the reaction of Western publics has apparently been to turn away increasingly from voting at all. Having examined the theoretical arguments about democracy in Part I, Part II will apply these to Britain in the twenty-first century to seek answers to the question of whether democracy works.

 What you should have learnt from reading this chapter

The argument over the meaning of democracy has been relentless, and this has been a very brief guide. One firm conclusion of Part I must be that it is quite futile to seek a winner in such a wide and often sterile debate. The task must be to distinguish the forms of democracy from one another to decide not which is 'genuine' nor even necessarily which is best (although you will have your own views on that) but the criteria by which they are distinctively characterised:

- **Democracy can be thought of either procedurally or idealistically:** that is, we can think of it in terms purely of its mechanical procedures – who can vote, how often elections are, and so on; or we can define it as a set of values and relationships, such as equality, popular control, and so on. This is akin to describing football in terms of the rules to be obeyed about numbers of players and size of nets, or in terms of the noble spirit of dynamic contest between teams, regardless of whether or not there are technical faults. 'Voting' wrote the idealist Fabian, G. D. H. Cole, 'is merely a handy device; it is not to be identified with democracy, which is a mental and moral relation of man to man.' Proceduralists such as Schumpeter do not regard democracy as having any inherent moral value, but rather as 'the institutional arrangement for arriving at political decisions in which individuals acquire the power to decide by means of a competitive struggle for the people's vote'; the idealistic view treats democracy as integrally moral and just – an end – whereas for proceduralists it is (or may be) merely a means to good government.

- **Democratic systems can be classified either by structure or by function.** Representative democracy and direct democracy are distinguished by the ways in which they are organised; protective democracy, competitive élitism and even liberal democracy are characterised by their aims in using any given structure (although aims may tend to suggest certain structures).

- **Democracy is not necessarily a perfect, or even a valuable, concept.** No ideology regards it as *per se* the best method of government for all people at all times: rather, they see it as serving certain ends or dealing best with certain sorts of question – or they simply describe whatever they aspire to as democracy: remember that, for all its reinterpretation in recent times, most regimes and thinkers during most of modern history would have shunned the term.

Having recognised all of the points above, we must now apply them to the claims made by modern British constitutionalists, academics and politicians. For the politics student, political theory is, after all, chiefly a means of organising, expressing and analysing opinions that surround everyday problems. To do that briefly is the purpose of Part II.

Glossary of key terms

Centralism Where power is transferred from a wider or more numerous set of people and institutions to a smaller, more concentrated group.

Communitarianism The belief that policy should be made by popular decision in small communities where practical duties and responsibilities are shared out as far as possible.

General Will The form of opinion which Rousseau believed would, under the right circumstances, emerge as the determining force in a participatory democracy. It would reflect the interests of citizens as a community rather than as sectional or isolated interests.

Iron Law of Oligarchy The principle developed by Robert Michels that the larger an organisation becomes, the greater its tendency to be dominated by a small number of potentially unrepresentative decision-makers at its top level.

Participatory democracy A system or process in which individual citizens participate directly in decision-making, by debating, questioning officials and voting on policy.

Pluralist Believing that an equilibrium or range of interests or power centres contributes, or should contribute, to the making of policy.

'Protective' democracy A system which uses popular opinion as a restraint against government inclined to invade individual liberties, but which also imposes limits on democratic decisions to prevent them invading civil liberties either. This prevents the so-called 'tyranny of the majority' or 'totalitarian democracy' feared by liberals.

Likely examination questions

1. Why did Madison, Mill and Schumpeter fear full democracy?

2. Is representative democracy a contradiction in terms?

3. Is direct public participation in decision-making either possible or wise?

4. 'One's view about the value of democracy is largely a reflection of one's view of human nature.' How true is this?

Helpful websites

Websites on political theory which go beyond encyclopaedia biographies without becoming challenging to the uninitiated are relatively rare. This one is part of the Political Studies Association's website, and gives a basic A–Z of political philosophers covering many mentioned in this chapter, as well as giving links to other sites such as that of the Rousseau Association:

www.psa.ac.uk/www/political_philosophy.htm

On the issues surrounding communitarianism, a good (though obviously not neutral) starting point is the websites of the Center for Communitarian Policy Studies at George Washington University in Washington, DC, where Amitai Etzioni is Director, that of Etzioni's own Communitarian Network:

www.gwu.edu/~icps/who.html

www.gwu.edu/~ccps/about_us.html

Suggestions for further reading

Blaug, R. and Schwarzmantel J., *Democracy: A Reader* (Edinburgh University Press, 2001).

Crick, B., *Democracy: A Very Short Introduction* (Oxford Paperbacks, 2002).

Eccleshall, R. et al., *Political Ideologies*, 3rd edn (Routledge, 2001).

Goodwin, B., *Using Political Ideas*, 4th edn (John Wiley, 1997).

Held, D., *Models of Democracy*, 2nd edn (Polity Press, 1996).

Heywood, A., *Political Theory: An Introduction* (Palgrave Macmillan, 2004).

Lively, J. and Lively, A., *Democracy in Britain: A Reader* (Blackwell, 1994).

On the historical process of democratic reform in the United Kingdom, the following is a good basic introduction:

Colin Pilkington, *The Rise of Representative Democracy in Britain* (Manchester University Press, 1997).

PART II: PRACTICE

CHAPTER 4

The Westminster Model

Contents

Overview

This chapter makes the case for the *status quo* in British politics: not in terms of who is in government, but in terms of how we are governed and, in particular, the case for the democratic character of our system. The main institutions and principles making up our constitution, and their development in recent history, are set out in order, and their democratic credentials reviewed using recent events as illustrations. As you read through, think of any other examples you regard as good illustrations of these arguments, and note any counter-arguments which occur to you, analysing the specific cases mentioned to show those criticisms. When you have read this chapter, you should have a good sense of why Britain is said to be democratic – and you may have started to see why some think it is not.

Key issues to be covered in this chapter

- What are the principal characteristics of the British parliamentary system?
- How and when did this system develop?
- How is this system said to be a democratic one?
- What recent examples of its effective operation can you identify?

Introduction

The Foreign Office publishes a series of booklets explaining in simple terms the central institutions and principles of public life in Britain. One of these, _British Democracy in Action_, asserts boldly that 'three essential freedoms sustain the British democratic way of life – free elections, freedom of speech, and open and equal treatment before the law'. This text reflects, albeit naïvely, the tradition which Professor Dennis Kavanagh has called the 'Britain is best' view, that permeated teaching about, and public attitudes to, the political system in the post-war era. This held that the 'Westminster model' of the British Constitution showed it to be effective in holding governments accountable to public opinion through the Commons, while making full use of the judgement of politicians and the expertise of civil servants, and protecting the rule of law through independent courts. It was in this confident spirit that the British Constitution was exported to former colonies, while reform of our system remained a non-issue at home.[1]

As late as the 1970s, politics students were told in R. M. Punnett's standard text book, _British Government and Politics_, that 'the overriding feature of the British system is that of mutual consent, and this alone justifies the claim that the system is fundamentally democratic', although Punnett's defence relied more heavily upon Britain's political culture than its constitutional system.[2] In the 1990s, leading commentator Professor (now Lord) Philip Norton claimed that 'our present system offers the values of accountability, coherence, flexibility and effectiveness, and I don't think anything else on offer matches those, and there's no evidence that the public actually believe in significant change to the constitution as a constitution'.[3] This outlook was expressed in the Conservative Party's manifesto of 1997, which asserted that 'alone in Europe, the history of the United Kingdom has been one of stability and security. We owe much of that to the strength and stability of our constitution – the institutions, traditions and laws that bind us together as a nation.' It also led to their opposition to constitutional reform in the Scottish, Welsh and regional English devolution referendums, to electoral reform, and to their scepticism about the Human Rights Act, still an explicit theme of their programme in 2005.

These days, however, this rosy view is not one accepted by all Britons, and a growing weight of academic analysis and public disillusionment has expressed Bill Jones's view that,

> the state of British democracy is not particularly healthy. We have an apathetic and disenchanted electorate, a legislative system which is creaking at the seams, a ruling elite in Westminster which is centralised, remote and tainted with repeated failure, a party system which is unrepresentative of much of the country and bankrupt of workable new ideas, a media which scarcely assists the democratic process, and an economy which has been ravaged by recession and may be in terminal decline.[4]

Since the 1960s, criticism of the traditional faith in our system has grown and, in the last decade, demands for reform have come from academic reports such as those of the Democratic Audit, from pressure groups such as Charter 88, and from journalists such as Simon Jenkins who concluded in 1995 that 'both governing parties in post-war Britain have had their chance to expand the range of democratic participation and diversify the accountability of government. Both have rejected that chance.'[5] Between 1973 and 1994, the proportion of people who told pollsters they were satisfied with the state of the country fell from 48 per cent to 28 per cent, while those agreeing that Britain is democratic dropped from 69 per cent in 1969 to 61 per cent. By then, barely half of voters under forty believed in British democracy.[6]

The parties themselves recognised, and felt, this public disillusionment, and experimented with new mechanisms for holding their own leaderships accountable. After 1997, the Labour governments embarked upon a programme of reform including devolution, electoral reform, legislation for freedom of information and human rights, and reform of the houses of Parliament, aimed at renewing British democracy. Yet the following two general elections saw the lowest turnouts of any since universal suffrage, and public trust in politicians appears dangerously scarce and fragile. In June 2005, YouGov found that 59 per cent of voters thought that 'most politicians have lost touch with ordinary people', and 63 per cent agreed with the statement 'whatever parties say during election campaigns, it's very hard to predict what will actually happen if they are elected'. Have decades of argument and campaign for reform, and three terms of reforming government, made any difference to the strength of Britain's claim to be a democracy?

The British Constitution

The British Constitution, as the least experienced of its students learn from the outset, is uncodified and largely flexible – that is to say that it is relatively easily changeable and, in some respects, its operating rules are even uncertain. The traditional view of the British Constitution, however, revolves around a number of central principles concerning the relationship between its main institutions, and argues that among those institutions, Parliament – and more especially the Commons as an elected body – is the most important. This is the Westminster, or liberal, model of the Constitution. It is impossible here to analyse any of those institutions in depth but what follows is a series of signposts to wider debates about the relationships between them. A swift survey of those relationships will serve for our purposes to illustrate the claim of Britain to be democratic.

The mandate

The central relationship of any representative democracy is the **mandate**, that is, the authority to govern given in trust from the public to their elected representatives at each election. As early as 1885, the famous jurist, A. V. Dicey, wrote in *Law of the Constitution* that, following the extension of the franchise to most men and equalisation of constituency sizes, political sovereignty now lay with the public, although the legal right to exercise power lay with the MPs whom they elected. More recently, this was the claim made on behalf of John Major after his 'endorsement' as Prime Minister in the election of 1992; likewise, the unprecedented surge in Labour support in 1997 led Tony Blair to assert that 'we were elected as New Labour, and we will govern as New Labour'. His claim to specific public endorsement for his own version of Labour policy was reiterated symbolically at Trimdon Labour Club in Sedgefield on the nights of the 2001 ('a big mandate for investment and change in our public services') and 2005 ('I feel proud . . . of what we can do with this mandate') general elections.

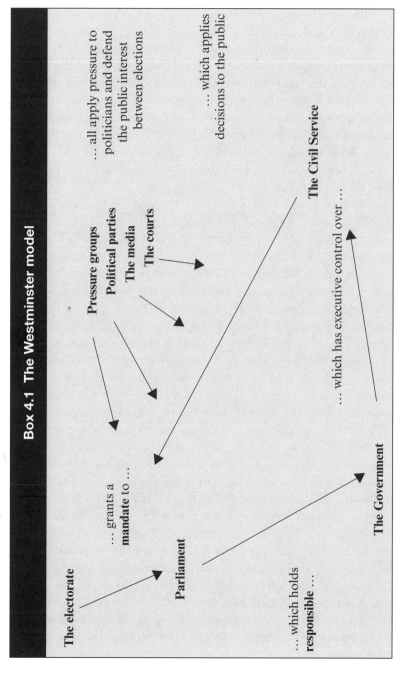

Box 4.1 The Westminster model

The electorate

... grants a
mandate to ....

Parliament

Pressure groups
Political parties
The media
The courts

... all apply pressure to
politicians and defend
the public interest
between elections

The Civil Service

... which applies
decisions to the public

... which has executive control over ...

... which holds
responsible ...

The Government

The claim of the British system to be a democracy rests upon this notion that, at elections, the British public freely determines who shall govern, and what their programme of government will be, by choosing between party groups with identifiable leaderships that would form alternative governments. The party reflecting the preference of the greatest number of voters then gains a parliamentary majority, and governs in the knowledge that its adherence to public opinion will be assessed at the next general election (this awareness was reflected in the Blair administration's early practice of issuing annual reports on the commitments of the Labour Party, and the extent to which they have been fulfilled).

The 1997 general election, which returned the Blair government to office, saw a record 3,724 candidates in the field, giving an average choice of 5.6 candidates in each constituency. The 2005 general election, with 5.4 per seat, comes close to matching this, and had 170 different recognised parties taking part, compared to eighty in 2001. A study of the 2005 election by the New Politics Network and the Joseph Rowntree Trust showed that candidates of the main parties had contacted the average voter just under twelve times, usually by leaflet or letter, but two in five voters had been spoken to personally by party activists by telephone or on the doorstep.[7] Though regulation of central party spending was introduced for the first time in 2001, registered parties still managed to get rid of £26.7 million during the campaign, a figure not incomparable to the £33.7 million spent by the three main parties in the whole year prior to the 1997 contest. At first glance, this ought to suggest that electors had a wide choice of candidates and parties, and plenty of opportunity to find out about their policies and leaders. This is especially true given the expanded nature of television news coverage and campaigning via the Internet, and using mobile telephones and text messaging at recent elections, and altogether this strengthens the claim of the winning party to a mandate. Even the newspaper which launched a campaign to change the electoral system after the 2005 result, the *Independent*, was forced to acknowledge on 10 May that it 'was probably a reasonable reflection of the people's will', and Liberal Democrat leader, Charles Kennedy, looked forward to 'a much healthier Parliament' in terms of representing the public's aspirations.

Parliamentary sovereignty

The second vital component of a representative democracy is that the representatives thus elected exercise power. In Britain, this is reflected in the doctrine of **Parliamentary sovereignty**, by which Parliament (dominated by the elected Commons) is the final law-making body in the country. Should any power be exercised – whether by government, corporation, company, or any other interest – over the public against its collective will, Parliament is legally empowered to act in the public interest and enforce the popular will.

Unlike the American Congress, Parliament is not ultimately constrained by courts, a written constitution or executive powers in its fulfilment of its democratic function. It was again A. V. Dicey who made explicit this convention that 'Parliament has the right to make or unmake any law whatever; and, further, that no person or body is recognised by the law of England as having a right to set aside the legislation of Parliament'. In the twentieth century, this was reasserted by Quintin Hogg, saying 'legally Parliament in omnipotent. It can do anything.'[8] Only laws made or acknowledged by Parliament apply in the United Kingdom, and any Parliament may undo the work of its predecessors or lesser authorities such as the courts or local councils. Parliament can remove governments (as it did to the Callaghan government in 1979), reject government legislation (as it did to Margaret Thatcher in 1986 and to John Major several times) and even alter government finances (as it did by refusing to authorise VAT on fuel proposed by Major). The Commons has, indeed, extended the scope of its power to some extent in recent years by demanding in 2003 the right to authorise war in Iraq – a decision made under Royal Prerogative by the Prime Minister and not previously discussed by Parliament in advance of military action). Throughout the parliamentary cycle, MPs and peers wring from ministers significant concessionary alterations to legislation on the threat of rejecting it, as they did with student tuition fees and identity cards.

Moreover, Parliament, especially the Commons, claims a certain moral authority, not only for the laws it passes, but also for the debates and proceedings it conducts. Its role as what Lloyd George called the 'sounding-board of the nation' was described more recently by John Major thus: 'It is our Parliament that is, and should be, at the centre of the democratic process. Parliament is where things happen. It is the voice of the people of Britain – it is the focus of the nation's unity at times of national grief or outrage. And it is the theatre for the grand convulsions of political history.'[9]

Ministerial responsibility

It is also essential to the 'Westminster model' to show that the executive – in this case, government ministers and their senior civil servants – is accountable to the sovereign Parliament. The conventions of collective **cabinet government** and individual ministerial responsibility are the guarantees of this. In British politics, members of governments are held, regardless of their personal opinions, to have consented to all aspects of government policy, and to be answerable for their outcomes. This requires ministers (and more recently parliamentary private secretaries, too) to defend government policy in public, and avoids those ministers undermining parliamentary democracy by mutual recrimination in the event of a policy proving unpopular. As long ago as 1867, it was evident to Walter Bagehot that Cabinet was the 'efficient' (today we would say 'effective') part of the Constitution; what is important is that the Cabinet is accountable to Parliament. Recent examples of cabinets 'toeing the line' against the better judgement of many of their members have included the Poll Tax under Mrs Thatcher, the 'wait and see' policy of John Major's government towards European economic and monetary union, and the continuation of the Millennium Dome project under Tony Blair. Notable examples of those who would not be held accountable for government policy, and therefore left the Cabinet, are Clare Short and Robin Cook, who – along with several junior ministers who also resigned – objected to government policy in Iraq at various stages of the war during 2003. Cook made it explicit that 'I can't accept collective responsibility for the decision to commit Britain now to military action in Iraq without international agreement or domestic support.'

Moreover, each minister is by convention accountable for the conduct of his or her own department, and the outcomes of its policies. The doctrine of individual ministerial responsibility was the basis of the resignations of Lord Carrington and John Nott following the invasion of the Falkland Islands in 1982, and of junior health minister Edwina Currie in 1988 after disquiet at the damage caused to farming by her remarks about salmonella in eggs. It may also be said to have contributed to the eventual resignation of former Chancellor, Norman Lamont, after the poor performance of the British economy, and his apparently bullish attitude to the situation. In a more general sense, too, it is necessary for a minister to maintain a constituency among MPs, and to put in competent performances at the dispatch-box. The failure to do this brought an end to the career of Thatcher favourite and erstwhile Social Security Secretary, John Moore, and might well have contributed to the curtailment of Harriet Harman's career in the same department in 1998. Peter Mandelson has the dubious distinction of having resigned twice over his personal conduct, both situations having at least some bearing upon his role as a minister: in December 1998 he left the post of Secretary for Trade and Industry after revelations that he owed money to Geoffrey Robinson, a ministerial colleague whose company the DTI was investigating (and who also resigned); in January 2001 he resigned as Northern Ireland Secretary after allegations that he had used his ministerial position to fast-track a passport application for wealthy Labour Party supporters the Hinduja brothers. The most apparently explicit recent case of resignation because of individual ministerial responsibility came with Estelle Morris, the Education Secretary, who left office in October 2002 following failure to achieve government targets in school literacy tests, and after controversy over the alleged interference of her department in the marking of A-level papers so as to guarantee politically acceptable results. Morris acknowledged her personal failure, saying: 'I have not done the job as well as I should have done'.

In addition to these conventions, ministers must observe the practices of answering questions in the Commons or Lords, of appearing before select committees, and must by convention themselves be members of one or other House of Parliament. These are the bonds that characterise the British Constitution as one of parliamentary rather than presidential or executive government. The day-to-day decision-making in a representative democracy may be in the hands of ministers rather than the public or even MPs; yet those ministers are reliant upon the support of MPs who are, in turn, reliant upon public support at future elections.

Accountable to ministers are the personnel of the senior Civil Service whose work it is to carry out the wishes of ministers endorsed by Parliament. The conventions of the 'Westminster model' suggest that civil servants occupy a position of neutrality, anonymity and permanence, allowing them to serve as advisers to contrasting governments, carrying forward experience and expertise, while taking no public responsibility for decisions made. These characteristics of the Civil Service – described by Professor Peter Hennessy as their 'DNA'[10] – were confirmed in the Fulton Report of 1968, and the neutrality of civil servants was reaffirmed by Cabinet Secretary, Richard Wilson, in a Radio Four interview in December 1999. As if to confirm its permanent and non-partisan character, the Civil Service's newly appointed most senior figure, the Cabinet Secretary, who took up office in June 2005, is Sir Gus O'Donnell, formerly John Major's Press Secretary, who first joined the Treasury Civil Service in 1979.

Judicial independence

The role of the judiciary in British constitutional theory is to be subordinate to Parliament, but independent of government and neutral in its judgements. The principle of parliamentary sovereignty indicates that judges cannot overrule, strike down or ignore parliamentary statutes, and so the judiciary is said to be subordinate to the democratic will of Parliament. Judges inevitably exercise discretion in interpreting those laws and in deciding sentences, however, and, in these matters, they are constitutionally bound to be politically impartial and independent of pressure from any sectional interests, thus satisfying the liberal democratic requirement for equality before the law. This is known as a 'technocratic' view of the judiciary's work, in which they are said to be guided by legal expertise and insight rather than personal attitudes or experiences. 'Every judge', claimed Master of the Rolls Lord Denning in 1980, 'on his appointment discards all politics and prejudices';[11] Lord Chief Justice Peter Taylor insisted in 1992 that 'the suggestion that judges are biased towards the Establishment does not stand up to examination'.[12] Indeed, judges have in recent years been increasingly active in considering issues of citizens' rights against government power in cases of judicial review, applications for which have increased from 160 per year in the mid-1970s to 2,886 twenty years later. Half of these cases – concerning everything from the government policy of slaughter during the foot-and-mouth crisis to local-authority boycotts of the Murdoch newspapers during the Wapping dispute, or the rights of asylum seekers facing deportation, are granted. Successful ones include cases reaffirming public right to information against the interest of government, such as the Matrix-Churchill affair, or guaranteeing access to legal aid, consultation by government departments or delaying the abolition of some elected local authorities. The law lords struck down a scheme proposed by Michael Howard as Home Secretary to cut the cost of criminal injuries compensation as 'mean, arbitrary and unjust', saying it was 'not only constitutionally dangerous but flies in the face of common sense'; Education Secretary David Blunkett was found to have neglected his obligations under the 1991 Education Act to consult throughout the education service before introducing his performance-related pay scheme in schools. The case delayed the scheme's introduction by six months. These are all examples of the continuing role of the courts under any government as the guarantor of the proper and equitable enforcement of democratic rights: in 1996, Lord Taylor justified **judicial activism** as an essential support to democracy, saying that 'the judiciary is here ensuring that the will of parliament is carried out'.[13]

Pluralism

The Foreign Office's description of British democracy alluded to in the introduction to this chapter says that 'a democratic society can only function properly when its citizens play an active part in its institutions', and goes on to stress the variety of occupational, religious and other pressure groups, as well as the media and voluntary wings of political parties that make this a reality. It was the government's reliance upon the co-operation of this constellation of interests and organisations, and the opportunities this relationship provides for the expression of public opinion between elections, that led Punnett to conclude that, despite the centralised and arcane structure of some British institutions, we live in a democracy because of 'the extent to which all Governments need the voluntary co-operation of the community as a whole'.[14] The existence of a pluralist dynamic in British politics – a rough equilibrium between competing major interests which brings pressure to bear on governments and allows the ready conveyance of public opinion to decision-makers – is an important part of Britain's claim to be democratic. Three groups of institutions offer British citizens the opportunity to participate in politics and influence the use of power between elections.

Parties

Edmund Burke said in 1775 that 'parties must ever exist in a free country' but, in Britain today, they are more than a necessary evil. Approaching a million people are individual members of political parties. In the cases of the major parties, this allows them to choose the leader by postal ballot, as more than 50,000 Liberal Democrats did to choose Charles Kennedy in 1999; over 300,000 Conservatives took part in the election of Iain Duncan Smith as their leader in 2001; and Tony Blair's mandate as Labour leader comes from nearly a million votes cast in the contest of 1994, counting those of affiliated trade union members. These polls were preceded by nationwide campaigns at party meetings and via the broadcast media and the press to convince party members of the merits – including the wider electoral popularity – of the candidates. Party members also have the opportunity to discuss and influence policy at annual party conferences and at more regular policy forums or council or executive meetings, and to hold MPs and councillors to account directly at these and local branch meetings. The Blair governments have been embarrassed by defeats at their own party conference on matters ranging from housing to pensions, student tuition fees and foundation hospitals. Tensions within the party over policy can also be aired and resolved through leadership rivalries and gestures, as with Gordon Brown's speech at the 2003 conference, ending with the insistence that 'we're best when we're Labour'. The draft of the successful 1997 Labour manifesto was even put to a postal ballot of all members, as was William Hague's decision to adopt a Eurosceptic policy towards the single currency in 1998. These decisions, of course, do not make government policy, nor even sometimes party policy; but they expose politicians to public criticism or to reports of public criticism from those who have been fighting elections on behalf of the party. Richard Kelly, for example, has argued that the extra-parliamentary Conservative Party had a significant influence upon party policy throughout 1979–97 through a network of contacts and conferences. In matters, such as provision for pensioners, criticism of the Blair government at conference has produced a clear reaction in subsequent government policy, in the form of real rises in the basic pension, free television licences and public transport, and giving impetus to the pensioners' Minimum Income Guarantee. Party structures are almost the only formal mechanism outside Parliament for challenging the leadership and direction of government. In a system which, by its nature, uses representative democracy, parties therefore play an important role in managing and conveying public opinion: hence Paul Webb's conclusion that 'it is precisely from the perspective of the participationist vision of democracy that political parties most often tend to be regarded as "failing" '.[15] Similarly, and confirming Burke, two-thirds of respondents to a British Election Study survey in 1997 responded positively to the statement 'Are parties necessary for the political system?'

Pressure groups

Pressure groups also play an important role in voicing opinions on which the parties are divided or ineffective. Governments of all parties have long maintained continuous liaison with significant organisations representing occupational, business or other collective interests, such as the National Farmers' Union, the TUC, the Confederation of British Industry, or the Law Society. But the involvement of pressure groups goes beyond sectional interests and large-scale corporatism and, in recent decades, the range and dynamism of pressure groups have flourished to become what Executive Director of Friends of the Earth, Charles Secrett, calls 'an invaluable expression of dissent. They are part of the life-blood of democracy'.[16] Issue groups – especially those involved with environmental policy such as Friends of the Earth or Greenpeace – have experienced a vastly increased membership and profile in recent years, giving huge numbers of citizens access to information, opportunities to participate and also some influence over government. Even the traditional journal, *The Economist*, went so far as to describe the animal rights movement as 'Britain's closest thing to a mass social movement'. There are in total some 350,000 voluntary organisations in Britain, about half of which are registered charities. Of course, many of these become explicitly politically active only periodically, as with the church organisations that support the Jubilee Debt Campaign to end Third World debts, or when Save the Children published critical reports on the progress towards government targets on elimination of child poverty in Britain in 2004 and 2005. Even the Women's Institute was in the political limelight briefly when its conference slow-handclapped Tony Blair's attempts to talk up investment in the NHS in 2000. A better guide to the number of organisations consistently lobbying government is the 7,000 registered in the Directory of British Associations, and the discovery by Rob Baggot in a survey of over 100 pressure groups in the 1990s that two-thirds had monthly contact with middle-ranking civil servants, and nearly half with junior ministers. Over a third had regular contact with cabinet ministers. Outsider groups, not enjoying this sort of contact, have in recent years succeeded in conveying public grievances to the government by mass protest and media coverage on everything from the Poll Tax to the work of the Child Support Agency, the Stephen Lawrence case, the abolition of fox-hunting and, perhaps most spectacularly, the war in Iraq, against which over a million people protested in London on 15 February 2003, and the Live 8 campaign led by celebrities from the worlds of music and film in July 2005 to urge G8 leaders to end world poverty. Not all of these secured the change in policy they wanted – indeed, in some cases, there were pressure groups on both sides – but few had no impact at all. John Rees of the 'Stop the War' coalition, for example, has argued that, without worldwide demonstrations against American foreign policy, there might have been an attempt to launch military action against Syria or Iran. The political costs Blair had already suffered made him keen to restrain Bush from further controversy. Rob Baggot concluded from his study that that 'modern democracy cannot exist without pressure groups. As channels of representation, they are as legitimate as the ballot box.'

The press, radio and television

The media are also an important instruments of pluralist liberal democracy. It is chiefly via the broadcast media, for example, that politicians are held accountable in public view on a day-to-day basis, and this has made public celebrities of figures such as Jeremy Paxman and John Humphrys for their aggressive pursuit of politicians under question. In an increasingly diverse and competitive media market-place, the pressure to respond to, reflect and engage public opinion has intensified in recent years for television, radio and the press alike. Britain is regularly claimed to have the population with the highest per caput readership of newspapers, and the range of mass-circulation papers covers most styles and political outlooks. Media scrutiny and criticism were responsible, at least in part, for the difficulties in, and departure from, office of John Major, David Blunkett, Estelle Morris, Peter Mandelson and Geoffrey Robinson. It is significant that Morris's contrite resignation acknowledged that 'I was not good at dealing with the modern media.' On policy issues, television and newspaper reports have repeatedly challenged government claims about the state of the NHS (in particular about hospital cleanliness) and also about the number and treatment of asylum seekers admitted to the United Kingdom. Other controversies on which the government has faced sustained criticism from the media include the costs and standards of the Millennium Dome project in 2000 and the tackling of the foot-and-mouth outbreak of 2001. It was certain elements of the press, rather than the main opposition party, that voiced the substantial opposition to war in Iraq in 2003, and the *Daily Mirror*, which lost considerable sales during its opposition to the war in 2003, felt obliged to shore up its populist appeal by purchasing the memoirs of Tony Martin, con-victed of killing an intruder to his home. Other papers have also shown themselves willing to reconsider their loyalties if they consider their readership is not satisfied with government, as in 1997 and 2001 when, for the first time, more than half of Britain's newspaper circulation was pro-Labour, and even Tory papers lost heart. (The *Sunday Times* edito-rial expressing support for John Major was entitled 'Tories, warts and all'.) The *Sun*, with some 4 million sales and 12 million readers, Britain's most popular newspaper, has veered from strong support for Thatcherism to endorsement of Tony Blair's Labour Party in 1997 and 2001. In 2005 the paper began with an open mind, merely urging elec-tors to use their vote, and later concluded that Labour remained the best option, and launched a particularly bitter attack on the Liberal Democrats. All of this suggests that the media are capable of playing a key role in shaping the political agenda, and are also susceptible to public opinion. Similarly positive conclusions have been reached in recent analysis of the media by Pippa Norris who, in 2000, identified a 'virtuous circle' of news coverage and civic engagement in politics.[18] A pioneering figure in liberal democratic thought and architect of the American Constitution, Thomas Jefferson famously remarked that 'were it left to me to decide whether we should have a government without newspapers, or newspapers without government, I would not hesitate to prefer the latter.' The Westminster model of British democracy certainly does not propose either option, but the role it allows the media is an important one for the reasons of investigation and representation argued above and implied by Jefferson.

Box 4.2 The Westminster model in action? The fall of Margaret Thatcher and its impact

Source A: Hugo Young, The Guardian, *23 November 1990*
'Finally the system, which says that this is cabinet and not prime ministerial government, reacted. There was a point beyond which it declined to be flouted. This point was identified by an age-old reflex: the perception that an election was about to be lost and power surrendered to the other side. No fear exceeds that of politicians faced with the loss of office, not even fear of the avenging virago across the table. So in the end, in a drama whose outlandishness aptly reflected the years before, she went.'

Source B: Alan Watkins, A Conservative Coup *(1992)*
'Her departure confounded the professors of politics. They had long maintained, certainly since the publication of Mackintosh's *The British Cabinet* in 1962, that the position of a Prime Minister in good health and with an adequate parliamentary majority was impregnable. To be fair to the academic observers, the circumstances of November 1990 may never be repeated. Nevertheless there is a lesson. It is imprudent to go around stating rules about prime ministerial power as if they must be true at all times and in all places. John Biffen said: "You know those maps on the Paris Metro that light up when you press a button to go from A to B? Well, it was like that. Someone pressed a button, and all the connections lit up." '

Source C: Anthony Seldon, Major: A Political Life *(1997)*
'The scope for strong, assertive leadership in the 1990s was less than in the 1980s. Not just was Major, as we have seen, a collegiate

leader, and such leaders do not make the weather, but he also faced far tougher Labour leaders than did Mrs Thatcher . . . Unlike Mrs Thatcher, and after the departure of Chris Patten, he never found a senior figure such as Whitelaw to underpin his position . . . Neither did Major have, like Mrs Thatcher, a coterie of sympathetic interpreters of his policies and position in the media and intellectual life – the *sine qua non* for a successful modern premiership . . . He felt peculiarly strongly the lack of a ready understanding of the problems he inherited from Thatcher, so reluctant was the press to admit to her having any faults. His first years were overshadowed by the recession and by the consequent problems in public finances (which he could have done more to master). His later years suffered because of a small and dwindling parliamentary majority at the mercy of eccentric backbenchers . . . In electoral terms, Major suffered from the emergence of New Labour, which stole the Tories' true secret weapon, not loyalty, but adaptability . . . The most difficult problem of all that he faced was that, with polls and by-elections pointing continually to the likelihood of a heavy defeat, there was little incentive for his own parliamentary party to follow his lead, when an alternative – any alternative – offered the prospect of a revival in fortunes.'

Source D: Graham P. Thomas, 'Has Prime Minister Major been replaced by President Blair?' in Lynton Robins and Bill Jones (eds), Debates in British Politics Today *(2000)*
'So far, this analysis describes the Blair "presidency", but as the sheen is wiped off the government Blair will need his colleagues to help shoulder the blame. The nature of government will become clearer as time passes. What is certain is that this essentially flexible and adaptable system accommodates both circumstances and personalities. No single model applies over time. "Events, dear boy, events" may produce something nearer to a collective system. Time will tell.'

Source E: Jon Smith, Election 2005 *(2005)*
'Camelot had come to Westminster. But Blair's loyal court is scattered now, and jealousies and rivalries inevitably flourished, even within it, in the intervening years. The Cabinet table, as he well knows, is not round but coffin-shaped. His children now have forever the memories of them bathed in sunshine with their father, as he walked into Labour history the moment he stepped back into No. 10 as the Queen's First Minister once more. It was a nice touch. But Blair knows that before long there will be those who seek to usurp him before he is ready to go, and are waiting to see him finally

walking out of that shiny black door. His election 2005 majority, though eminently workable, had left him wounded and vulnerable to rebellion, if not open revolt. That drama has yet to unfold. Things can only get bitter.'

How effectively democratic are the pressures that forced Margaret Thatcher's resignation, and to what extent have they come to bear on her successors?

 What you should have learnt from reading this chapter

- What has been described in this chapter is the patriot's view of democratic Britain: a sophisticated, adaptable and enduring system of representative democracy in which public opinion drives the sovereign institution to bend government policy to its purpose. As a representative system, of course, it gives due weight to the expertise of bureaucrats, judges and legislators but, on key issues, the force of public consensus cannot be resisted, even between elections. The system, its admirers might contend, does not work equally effectively all the time – but it is the imperfections of the system that lead to disillusionment, not its normal operation. When it works, it works well: it relies upon a rough equilibrium of contrasting forces seeking a balance of leadership and stability within the general context of public control.

- A favourite metaphor of conservative thinkers since the Enlightenment may be appropriate here: the Westminster model is like a living organism – the body politic, as it were. It adapts and evolves slowly and naturally; each organ, or part of the system, has a role to play; at times one part (say, the opposition parties) is weak, and so another (such as the Prime Minister) grows unusually strong in compensation. Yet this is usually reversed over the course of time. This is illustrated by the case of Margaret Thatcher (see Box 4.2, above): regarded as one of the most dominant of all Prime Ministers, she was forced to resign following a string of parliamentary by-election and council election defeats, violent public protests against the poll tax, the resignation of her own Chancellor and Deputy Prime Minister and the desertion of media supporters such the *Sunday Times*. Subsequent Prime Ministers have lived in the shadow of that episode. Most significantly (as conservatives from Burke onwards always gravely stressed), sudden, artificial change or removal of any one organ of the system is unnecessary and might endanger the whole system.

- The defenders of the Westminster model are still to be found, but Kavanagh is right to say that they are less numerous and less uncritical than during the post-war era. The Conservatives' forlorn attempts to resist constitutional reform at succeeding elections and referendums from 1997 onwards are one sign of that. So how has this self-contained and democratic conception of the British Constitution come to be regarded as redundant – and what alternative methods of government might there be? To these issues we turn in the remaining chapters.

Glossary of key terms

Cabinet government A type of government the policies of which are made by open and equal discussion among the Cabinet members, and which is held accountable collectively for those policies.

Judicial activism Intervention by courts in decisions which politicians regard as proper for elected or accountable figures. This includes the use of judicial review, the Human Rights Act or European Union law to delay or strike down ministerial decisions.

Judicial independence The rule that the decisions of courts in sentencing or arriving at verdicts or other conclusions should be based upon legal precedent and principles rather than pressure from any political source, particularly the government.

Mandate The right to govern because of public support for the personnel of the government and its policies, usually expressed in an election.

Parliamentary sovereignty The doctrine that the current Parliament ultimately controls law inside the United Kingdom, even if its powers are passed temporarily or conditionally to other institutions.

Likely examination questions

From where might the British government claim its mandate?

What is meant by 'parliamentary government' in the context of the United Kingdom?

What part does the judiciary play in maintaining liberal democracy in the United Kingdom?

Which non-governmental institutions and processes contribute to British democracy and how?

Helpful websites

Three official websites giving extensive information on the structure and activity of government in Britain are these:

www.parliament.uk/

www.direct.gov.uk/Gtgl1/GuideToGovernment/fs/en

www.cabinetoffice.gov.uk/

The following is a basic factual educational site which deals with some of the key concepts in this chapter:

www.historylearningsite.co.uk/british_constitution.htm

On the work of the parties, a positive explanation can be gained from each party's website, namely www.labour.org.uk/home; www.conservatives.com/; and www.libdems.org.uk/. For the work of pressure groups, as you can imagine, there are thousands of individual groups' sites which will give details of their campaigns.

 ## Suggestions for further reading

Old standards, such as R. M. Punnett's *British Government and Politics*, or J. Harvey and L. Bather's *The British Constitution*, have not been reissued for well over ten years, and so are of limited use even as a statement of the traditional view. The following are more recently updated but very well-established texts offering a conventional account of the key features of the British constitution:

Anthony H. Birch, *The British System of Government*, 10th edn (Routledge, 1998).

Philip Norton, *The British Polity*, 4th edn (Longman, 2000).

A briefer text with a legal flavour but which covers recent constitutional changes and provides some European context is:

Hilaire Barnett, *Britain Unwrapped* (Penguin, 2002).

This last title is a colossal study embracing contributions from a wide field of eminent authors:

Vernon Bogdanor (ed.), *The British Constitution in the Twentieth Century* (British Academy Centenary Monographs, 2002).

Critiques of British Democracy

Contents

Overview

This chapter explains and discusses some of the main criticisms of Britain's political system – particularly the criticisms from those who do not regard it as democratic enough. These are categorised by reference to the same principles and relationships as were used to set out the system's positive features in Chapter 4, but here those relationships and claims are brought into question. These criticisms will be illustrated using recent evidence of the operation of the political system, and will refer to some of the main organisations and individuals who have voiced those criticisms. Keep in mind not only the strength you regard these criticisms as having but also the changes they imply would make Britain more democratic – and whether, even if that is true, it would make Britain better governed.

Key issues to be covered in this chapter

- What criticisms are made of the British system of government's claim to be democratic?
- Who has made these criticisms?
- Why has criticism of the British system become more commonplace recently?
- Are these criticisms likely to grow or decline in the future?

The British political system

Questions were first raised about the 'Britain is best' view of our political system in the 1960s, and these became more commonplace in the 1970s and 1980s. These criticisms spawned (or gave impetus to) a wealth of reports and books, and parties, such as the Nationalists, Greens and Social Democrats, and pressure groups including Charter 88 and the Hansard Society, expressing discontent. Confidence in our existing Constitution was symbolically rejected by the electorate in 1997 when John Major made 'the defence of the Union' a principal plank of his election manifesto, and won the lowest Conservative share of the vote since 1832. An important feature of this body of criticism is the increasing diversity of the sources from which it came, whether in terms of location on the political spectrum, style of protest, or exact objection. The common feature of these arguments was the belief that relationships within the Westminster model were not as traditionally supposed: they were, and are, myths rather than fundamental principles; failed mechanisms for democracy – or even cynical substitutes for it – rather than active, effective vehicles of public opinion.

The mandate: three problems

The insistence of the *Sunday Times* on 4 May 1997 that 'for many people the Labour mandate was a qualified one' is a sign that doubt about the probity of the electoral process in Britain is not confined to radical quarters. The ideas that the results of general elections in Britain reflect public opinion, and that politicians live in fear of the next contest, are derided for various reasons.

First past the post

The most immediately obvious cause of this derision is the eccentric British electoral system. Used by few countries which are not former British colonies, and adopted by none of the new democratising states in Eastern Europe, it allows a single party to rule uninhibited with only a minority – and sometimes not the largest minority – of the votes cast. Large areas of the country are turned into what the Jenkins

Commission called 'electoral deserts',[1] in which, despite winning many votes, a party secures no seats at all (this was true of Labour in the south-east outside London in the 1980s, and of the Tories in Wales and Scotland in 1997). Lastly, each citizen has only one MP, only a minority of whose constituents need have voted for him or her.

In the 1950s and early 1960s, this was less evident as a problem because, with two evenly matched parties, each with large shares of the vote relatively broadly spread across the country, parliamentary results in which they gained 98 per cent of seats for 96 per cent of the vote were perceived as reasonable. With the development of a more fragmented and volatile party system at the electoral level, however, the first-past-the-post system has proved incapable of reflecting, even roughly, the wishes of the public. Governments have been formed on less than 40 per cent of the vote; parties with 25 per cent of the vote have won only 3.5 per cent of the seats; and governments with a declining minority of the poll have won an increased majority in the Commons. Even Labour's 1997 'landslide' victory was secured despite the active opposition of nearly 56 per cent of those who voted.

It was in the wake of the 1974 elections, which had seen a minority Labour government elected on fewer votes than the Conservatives, that S. E. Finer wrote in *Adversary Politics and Electoral Reform* (1975) that 'for a government to claim a "mandate" to carry out its policy, it ought to be elected by at least half the votes'.[2] After the 1983 election, petitions of over a million signatures demanding a referendum on electoral reform were delivered to Parliament by the cross-party Campaign for Fair Votes and, in the 1990s, the Labour Party appointed a party commission under Professor (now Lord) Raymond Plant to examine the possible alternatives, following which Labour policy approved changes to provide for proportional representation in new assemblies for Scotland, Wales, London and for European Parliament elections. The Blair government also established the Jenkins Commission to design an alternative to first past the post for elections to the Commons. Though it reported in 1998, Blair has refused to commit his government to holding the referendum on its findings promised in Labour's 1997 manifesto either before or after the next general election. Thus, the sovereign body of the British system is likely to continue to be elected by a body which, in Professor Vernon Bogdanor's assessment, 'fails to perform either of the two functions required of an electoral system. It gives power not to the majority but to the strongest minority; and it fails to ensure that all significant minorities are properly represented.'[3]

Never were the weaknesses of the electoral system better illustrated than at the 2005 general election. The Labour Party, with little more than a third of the votes cast, formed a government with a healthy parliamentary majority; the Conservatives, with almost exactly the same share of the national vote as at the previous election, made some thirty-six gains in a smaller House of Commons; the Liberal Democrats, of course, with their geographically even spread of votes, had less than one in ten of the seats for more than one in five of the votes; and three parties with hundreds of thousands of votes, namely UKIP (605, 973), the Greens (257, 695) and the British National Party (192, 746) secured no representation whatsoever, although their supporters could have made up the entire electorate (let alone the plurality of those voting) of well over a dozen constituencies. The election of a government on such a limited mandate led one national newspaper, *The Independent*, to launch a campaign to demand the issue of electoral reform for the House of Commons be revived, declaring that the election constituted a 'travesty of democracy'. Its editorial commentary on 10 May linked this objection to wider contemporary democratic issues:

> The election campaign has been notable for a persistent unease, widely expressed by voters of all parties, about British democracy. Areas of concern have included: marginalisation of Parliament, ballot fraud, voter alienation, the Prime Minister's presidential style, the erosion of civil liberties such as habeas corpus and jury trial, compulsory ID cards, the absence of a written constitution, and an electoral system that deprives millions of voters of a meaningful say in the composition of their government. Some would say our democracy is in crisis; few would dispute it is in urgent need of a health check.

Voter disillusionment

There are more fundamental problems than this, however, for the technical weaknesses of the electoral system merely serve to mask a pattern of growing public disillusionment with the main parties, the choices they offer, and indeed the value of voting at all. The party system of the 1950s and 1960s offered voters a clear choice between two main contending alternative governments with enough common ground to sustain stable constitutional government, but a distinctness of history, values, policies and social character that allowed for a clear choice at elections. Since then, the main parties have become volatile, and at times ineffectual, and this has been reflected in the public's reaction.

In the mid-1970s, both main parties began a process of polarisation in which the Conservatives adopted policies of low taxation, widespread privatisation, radical welfare reform and a strident Anglo-American approach to foreign affairs, while Labour proposed unilateral nuclear disarmament, nationalisation of hundreds of large commercial interests, higher levels of direct taxation and withdrawal from the European Economic Community. During the 1990s, however, the main parties converged on almost identical political ground so that, in 1997, official party policies became virtually indistinguishable on key issues such as Europe, taxation and public ownership. 'With some legitimacy' ran one leading commentary on the 1997 general election, 'the Conservatives might claim that many of their clothes had been stolen . . . Labour's managerial approach to policy issues signified a decisive break with its ideologically driven approach of former years.'[4] Needless to say, this convergence made the internal discipline of each of the parties more difficult, and the 1980s and 1990s were marked by regular defections from, and challenges to the leadership of, Labour and the Conservatives. In December 2002, Transport and General Workers' Union leader Bill Morris said that 'the dividing line between our parties seems to be blurred if not erased altogether', and he accused Labour as acting as a 'pathfinder for future Tory policies' such as foundation hospitals and university top-up fees.

These developments contributed to a situation in which many traditional supporters of the two main parties no longer felt represented by them, and their joint share of the vote at general elections accordingly fell from 91.3 per cent during 1945–70 to 75.0 per cent thereafter. Labour reached a low point of 27 per cent in 1983, while the Conservatives were reduced to 31 per cent of the vote in 1997. The loyalty of these remaining voters also waned and, by the 1990s, pollsters found only half the number of 'very strong identifiers' (loyal voters who hardly ever consider deserting for another party) for each of the main parties that there had been in the early 1960s. Since 1997 this process has accelerated, with the two main parties being reduced to 64 per cent of the vote between them at the European Parliament elections of June 1999, and less than half of the total vote cast in the same elections in 2004. The year 2005 saw the lowest joint vote of the two main parties at a general election since 1945. Thus, the winning party has gained office on a smaller and smaller minority of the vote – but partly because its chief opponent has also failed to connect with the public.

During the years of Conservative rule from 1979 to 1997, a concern grew up among writers such as Professor Anthony King that Britain was experiencing 'one-party', or, more exactly, '**dominant-party**' government, in which – though many parties contested elections – only one had the distribution and level of support to win. It was feared that the distinction between the party of government and the institutions of the state such as the Civil Service, public broadcasting and the courts was becoming blurred, and that other parties were becom-

---

Box 5.1 Joint Labour and Conservative Party percentage vote share at recent general and European elections

	General elections	European elections
1979	80.9	83.8
1983	70.0	
1984		77.3
1987	73.1	
1989		74.6
1992	76.3	
1994		74.8
1997	73.9	
1999		63.8
2001	72.4	
2004		49.3
2005	67.6	

What does the sharp decline in support for the two main parties in the last 25 years signify?

ing demoralised, or alternatively copied the winning party so as to offer the public no real choice at all. It might be argued that Labour now enjoys a similar position of dominance over a quiescent Conservative Party; or, more sinister still, it could be said that the transformation of Labour's policies in the 1990s changed Britain from a one-party state to a one-doctrine state – and neither is particularly democratic. This, indeed, was the origin of the dilemma underpinning long-serving Labour activist John Harris's book *So Now Who do we Vote For?*.[5] The central issue for a critical assessment of the Westminster model is that the mandate of a government relies upon widespread support in the face of distinctive and realistic opposition. It is becoming doubtful whether any of those conditions apply to modern Britain.

What does the vote mean?

Ultimately, the mandate is bound to be an elusive shibboleth because it rests upon presumptions about what was intended by those voting, and what they wished their vote to signify. This, of course, is a matter that psephologists have never been able conclusively to resolve, partly because voters may not be willing to tell analysts; they may not be entirely sure themselves of the combination of motives that determined their vote; or indeed, the causes may be of a fundamental sociopsychological nature, such as class identity or family upbringing, of which voters themselves are not even aware.

In the context of the 2005 general election, for example, it is not certain whether even those citizens who voted Labour (even excluding those Liberal Democrats who voted tactically to dislodge the Tories) were expressing approval of Tony Blair's leadership or that of his Cabinet, or in the expectation that Blair would resign, as he had promised, and that he would be replaced by Gordon Brown. Were Labour voters showing support for their party's policies on taxation, welfare, fox-hunting, nuclear power, immigration and asylum, constitutional reform, law and order, the arts or foreign affairs? We know what issues the public told pollsters they thought important, but that does not tell us whether the public was aware of, or honest about, their own sense of priorities: does 'Iraq' as an issue refer to the occupation of Iraq, or the distrust the voter feels of Blair because of the manner in which we were brought into the conflict, and which is echoed in disappointment over Labour's record on other policy issues such as welfare? We do not even know whether policy issues as a whole were the deciding factor. Voters may, for example, have been convinced by the state of the economy, or socially or sentimentally loyal to the Labour Party for decades before Blair became leader, and have shared none of the enthusiasms of 'New' Labour. They may have had reason to support the local candidate where they would not have voted for other candidates of the same party. Finally, they may have been moved mainly by a negative desire to punish the Conservatives, or merely a vague fear about what a Conservative government would do.

Though opinion polls and anecdotal evidence will point to some of these as being more important than others, and the Labour campaign in 2005 specifically highlighted six pledges, it is never possible to say with cast-iron certainty that a government has 'broken' its mandate as Blair's was accused of doing over higher education tuition fees, lone parents' benefits or the promised referendum over electoral reform. It is always possible that another promise (say a fiscal one) takes priority, or that the promise had no timetable, or that the promise was not the one that caused voters to support the government, or indeed that the electorate has changed its mind. It is impossible even to say with certainty which policies voters are aware of: we do know, however, that a third of voters claim never to watch party political broadcasts, and that only about 3 per cent (probably accounted for by party members and others with a professional interest) read any party manifesto.

We are left, therefore, hoping that general elections generate and realise in government a collective spirit of the public, a clear instruction as to what elected politicians are to do – a sort of indirect representation (though, of course, Rousseau denied such a thing was possible) of the General Will. We are certainly told by politicians on the winning team that this is what has happened at elections. But we know that voters' behaviour is more complex than that. It is that uncertainty that allows politicians plausibly to assign themselves a mandate to do those things they wish to do, and to disclaim any uncomfortable obligations. In reality, the Labour mandate of 1997 may consist of little more than an injunction to be unlike the previous government – and some have found them wanting even in this. Subsequent election victories can reasonably be taken to suggest that the voting public collectively did not want the Conservatives to return to office, but little more; and, of course, the voting public was a much reduced share of the electorate in 2001 and 2005. This idea of a 'doctor's mandate' merely to govern competently and with good intentions would seem to confirm the views of Madison, Schumpeter and even Mill about the limited potential of democracy. We must ask ourselves: is it because of British institutions that British democracy has failed, or is it because of democracy?

Parliamentary sovereignty

Even if we leave aside the problems of the process of election, the almost universal experience of the MPs thus elected is one of initial disappointment at the limited nature of their powers. They come down from the euphoria of election to find that the public's political sovereignty, of which they are in theory the trustees, is, in fact, held in any number of places other than the Palace of Westminster. Long-serving MP Brian Sedgemore concludes his introductory guide to Parliament thus:

> When you first entered the House of Commons you were told 'Parliament rules OK', but warned that things are not always as they seem. Now you are a position to know that Parliament's omnipotence is a myth put about by constitutional theorists, and that only two things can be said with certainty about parliamentary democracy in Britain today. First, effective power does not reside in Parliament or with MPs. Secondly, there is little that is democratic about the exercise of that power.[6]

Another Labour veteran MP, and a former politics lecturer, Austin Mitchell, agreed that 'People and parliamentarians both comfort themselves in their decline with the myths of the past.' Nor is this pessimism the exclusive property of left-wing MPs: it was leading Conservative Lord Hailsham who, in 1976, gave to political analysis the term '**Elective Dictatorship**' when, in the Dimbleby Lecture, he accused the executive of making arbitrary and undemocratic decisions without parliamentary approval. In 1990, he described *The Purpose of Parliament*, the book in which he had attributed legal omnipotence to Parliament, as 'now only of doubtful value'.[7] By

1994, Tory MP Andrew Rowe acknowledged that, in the Commons, 'a feeling of powerlessness is everywhere: MPs feel sidelined and ineffective; it's too easy for the government to ignore them. The public senses their uselessness.' Academics studying the role of Parliament have, under the Blair governments, gone so far as to describe Labour MPs as 'Daleks', pointing to their whips' thoroughgoing use of model speeches, questionnaires and press releases.[8] Looking at the subject from a longer historical perspective, Bruce Lenman wrote in 1992 that 'despite the windy rhetoric of politicians with liberty on their lips and power in their hearts, the UK government by the second half of the twentieth century was neither a parliamentary one, nor a particularly democratic one'.[9] What is it that causes such levity and despondency among commentators and among parliamentarians?

The power of the whips

MPs routinely complain that a variety of interlopers has stolen the power of Parliament, causing a so-called '**democratic deficit**': pressure groups, the European Union, business interests and the media are among the most commonly named culprits, but the executive is always in some way complicit in the theft as the handler of the stolen goods, and often are themselves the beneficiaries. It is through the Whips' Office that governments (and, less effectively, leaders of the Opposition) exert discipline over their MPs. Through them, often condemned by back-benchers as 'bully boys', the government effectively controls the agenda and the outcome of parliamentary discussion.

Around 50 per cent of the timetable of the Commons is occupied with government legislation, the content and priority of which are decided in Cabinet. After allowing time for questions to ministers, and standing and select committees, less than 5 per cent of Commons time (and usually the most inconvenient slots) is devoted to private members' bills, most of which will be voted down or talked out without the support of the government. Thus, MPs have little opportunity to make an individual contribution to legislation, beyond the gesturing effect of early day motions and adjournment debates.

When a parliamentary division does take place (generally on government bills or opposition resolutions), MPs have little opportunity to exercise discretion: if the Whips' Office issues a three-line whip, MPs will find that their treasured place on a favourite select committee, their pairing arrangement with an opposite number, and even their long-term career are on the line if they defy the government's instructions. In back-bench rebellions against the whips over charges for dental and eye tests (1988) and the ratification of the Maastricht Treaty (1993), Conservative Prime Ministers Margaret Thatcher and John Major were accused in the press by their own MPs of having the whips bully and coerce back-benchers into supporting the government. Within six days of their 1997 victory, Tony Blair told the Parliamentary Labour Party's first meeting that 'the parliamentary party was not elected to obstruct the government's mandate', and New Labour MPs, made to sign a code of conduct promising not to 'bring the party into disrepute', were provided with electronic pagers to remind them when and how to attend, submit questions and vote (see Box 1.2, Chapter 1). At the end of the first session of the Blair government, Philip Cowley showed that 'Labour MPs are currently rebelling infrequently, in both absolute terms and in comparison with most of the recent parliaments' and that 'there are few surprise names amongst those who choose to rebel'.[10]

Under the second Blair government, the Commons proved more turbulent as the policies of the government became more controversial and less clearly authorised by public mandate. Nonetheless, the government's managers succeeded in securing the passage of legislation making possible the introduction of higher university tuition fees, foundation hospitals and Anti-Social Behaviour Orders. Most controversially of all, the Commons voted in favour of British participation in military action in Iraq. It must be said that each of these outcomes represented the effect of several features of the Westminster model – the electoral system and, in the case of Iraq, the party system – giving questionable democratic service as well as the failings of the Commons itself; however, it is a measure of the effectiveness of the government whips that, though nearly 200 Labour MPs signed an early day motion against higher student tuition fees in 2003, not enough carried this through to voting against the measure to block it. It was during this Parliament that one Labour MP, Paul Marsden, defected to the Liberal Democrats, complaining of physical intimidation at the hands of the whips.

As far as democratic government is concerned here, the issue is whether it is democratic for party leaders effectively to compel MPs (whose place in Parliament relies heavily upon the support of those leaders) to vote against what they regard as their judgement of their constituents' wishes or interests, their local party's preferences, their personal judgement, the opinion of the general public, the interests of the nation, or any combination of these? There are certainly those who would argue that, even if the Commons were democratically elected, its power is so reduced that it is an image rather than an engine of democracy. Within three years of the Blair government taking office, Labour MP and Chairman of the Public Administration Committee, Tony Wright, wrote anxiously about 'the intensification of party management and the strengthening of central direction within government' saying that 'with party control at its zenith, Parliament is unlikely to be let off the leash'.

The House of Lords

It goes without saying that the House of Lords continues to be an obstacle – however limited – to a democratic system. Though its members are entirely unelected and unaccountable to the public in any formal way, it nonetheless initiates, discusses and delays legislation. Since Blair came to office, it has put back at least one government proposition (the equalisation of the age of consent for homosexual and heterosexual men) by over a year. The Lords claimed then to be acting democratically because their action was in accordance with many opinion polls measuring public sentiments at the time: they also reversed an overwhelming free vote in the Commons, however. Similar claims were made when the Lords delayed the prohibition of fox-hunting until 2004. More fundamentally, however, coincidence between the opinions of one group of people and another is not in itself democratic: whether in the procedural or the idealistic conception of democracy, it is the relationship between government and citizenry (either electoral or more abstract) that characterises democracy, and no such relationship exists between the British citizenry and the Lords. A better description of that relationship might be paternalism. There may be arguments for the House of Lords, in its current or recent forms, but none of these arguments is a democratic one.

Ministerial responsibility: two problems

If the elected body of the Commons is not in itself powerful, can it at least control those who are? The doctrine of cabinet government suggests that it can; much recent analysis concludes, however, that this is misleading.

Prime ministerial government

First of all, the presumption that the Cabinet meets regularly and decides government policy collectively is naive. The membership, frequency, agenda and conclusions of cabinet meetings are determined by the Prime Minister, and ministers since Richard Crossman have complained that this gives other cabinet members little control over the direction of government policy. 'The full Cabinet' commented John Nott, Mrs Thatcher's Defence Secretary, 'was never more than a rubber stamp.'[11] Tony Blair has now limited Cabinet to a once-weekly meeting, sometimes no more than forty minutes long, at which the Prime Minister is not always present. Close aides of the Prime Minister, such as former Press Secretary Alastair Campbell, are widely held to be far more influential in crafting government policy than most cabinet ministers, and former deputy leader of the Labour Party, Lord Hattersley, recently remarked that 'Cabinet government has been dying for 40 years in the country. I'm not sure it's dead yet, but Tony is very near to giving it a lethal injection.'[12] Even in what is an unusually harmonious Cabinet, constructed with an unusually free hand, difficult ministers have on occasion been removed (Frank Field) or marginalised (John Prescott); favourites who are obliged to leave office soon return (Harriet Harman, David Blunkett), some more than once (Peter Mandelson). Despite the important role of ministers in bilateral or informal meetings with the PM, and notwithstanding the constraints that Cabinet can under some circumstances (such as a divided party) impose, Michael Foley's study of the role of the head of government in the 1990s concluded that 'it is no exaggeration to declare that British premiership has to all intents and purposes turned into an authentically **British presidency**'.[13]

If these criticisms have substance, it is not through parliamentary control of the Cabinet that government is democratically accountable, but through a much more remote and generalised relationship between the Prime Minister and the electorate, as Foley claims. Necessarily, this is a far less detailed sort of control, and indeed the Prime Minister, not being directly elected, may not enjoy the support of electors as much as alternative leaders. This is at best, again, a Schumpeterian sort of democracy which installs leadership figures with broad aims for the medium term, and lets them get on with it. The question for this enquiry is whether any different sort of arrangement is either possible or desirable.

Civil Service reform

The second difficulty in holding the executive to account is the changed nature of the Civil Service. The theory of Civil Service neutrality was always held in doubt by politicians: left-wing radicals, such as Tony Benn, saw them as unsympathetic to the Labour programme and the trade unions because of their class background, and claimed that his Permanent Secretary, Sir Anthony Part, obstructed his attempts to fulfil manifesto promises on nationalisation. Margaret Thatcher, by contrast, believed that the bureaucracy had a vested interest in an over-large state, that it was invulnerable to the market pressures which kept industry efficient, and that in the eleven years of Labour government between 1964 and 1979, the Civil Service had internalised too many socialist values, and come to accept economic decline. In both parties, therefore, there was suspicion that the Civil Service obstructed the implementation of popular policies that formed part of the government's mandate.

The reforms of the Civil Service which have taken place since may have made matters worse, however. From the outset, Thatcher took a keen interest in the appointment of permanent secretaries, with the acknowledged purpose of eliminating the sort of obstructiveness she had experienced as Education Secretary. The total number of civil servants has been cut by a third, and many of their functions have been privatised. Most of the remaining activities of the Civil Service have been split between executive agencies following the 'Next Steps' report issued by Sir Robin Ibbs in 1988, and work to much more exact instructions, targets and financial constraints than in the past. The chief executives of these agencies are also now publicly recognisable figures in a way their predecessors never were, appearing before parliamentary select committees and in television interviews.

In some respects, this managerial culture of relations between ministers and civil servants could be an advance for democracy, ensuring that policy objectives are pursued more fully and promptly than in the past. And there is evidence that the Blair government has continued this expectation of the Civil Service, even to the point of being accused by the Civil Service union, the First Division Association, of 'bullying' its members. This more uncritical style of administration may give rise to rash or ill-considered legislation, such as the Poll Tax, by neglecting the experience, but this is not a problem of inadequate democracy – it may be a problem of too much, in fact. Of course, policies such as the Poll Tax may or may not have carried a mandate (it was included in the 1987 Conservative manifesto, after all) but that problem, as we have already seen, lies elsewhere in the system. The democratic problem raised by Civil Service reform is the loss of anonymity: the public visibility of senior civil servants has allowed ministers to direct attention and blame to them when public opinion is displeased with the operation of government. Well-known examples of this include the departure of Derek Lewis as head of the Prison Service under Home Secretary Michael Howard in October 1995 following the Learmont Report on the state of prisons; the resignation of Ros Hepplewhite as Chief Executive of the Child Support Agency after critical reports from the Social Security Select Committee; and most recently the castigation by the Foreign Affairs Select Committee of Permanent Secretary Sir John Kerr over the Sandline affair in 1999.

In each of these cases, it could be argued that civil servants drew fire from the nominally democratically accountable ministers in their departments. The theory of individual ministerial responsibility has evidently been increasingly irrelevant as the responsibilities of government grew in the twentieth century, and therefore the ability of ministers to supervise civil servants was reduced. Yet the changes of the last twenty years of that century made a qualitative difference to the control of Parliament over public policy, a view confirmed in the conclusions of Colin Campbell and Graham Wilson's study *The End of Whitehall* (1995).[14] The twenty-first century has opened with the British executive more centralised and less accountable than before. In part this may be a necessity, but it is hardly a democratic one.

Judicial independence

The role of the courts, like that of the Civil Service, has always been an equivocal one from a democratic point of view. Like the Civil Service, the courts are unelected and unaccountable. At best, they may be said to represent the liberal part of liberal democracy which sees the rule of law and the preservation of individual rights against government as integral to meaningful democracy. The success of British courts in fulfilling this role has always been disputed but, in the latter years of the twentieth century, they began to assume another role, and to attract renewed criticism as a result.

The traditional critique of the English judiciary has been that, because of its social composition, it cannot dispense justice equitably in those cases that involve conflicts between the interests of citizens with their background, and those without. Specifically, being in four cases out of five the products of public school and Oxbridge educations, and being almost exclusively white and male, judges in the high court and upwards are not sympathetic to the problems and needs of most British people. This was the conclusion drawn by Professor J. A. G. Griffith in his study, *The Politics of the Judiciary*, first published in 1977.[15] This suggested that the function of guaranteeing equal access to justice was not being carried out and that, rather than being 'technocratic' in their application of the law, judges are necessarily 'political', that is to say, they make judgements that inevitably involve value judgements about political issues and interests, and are guided in these by their own opinions and experiences.

In the 1980s and 1990s, however, the criticism of the judiciary came from different quarters. As Lord Justice Taylor's remarks, cited in Chapter 4, indicate, judges became increasingly embroiled in disputes with the Conservative governments of the period, granting judicial review of government decisions in fields ranging from defence to education, immigration to social security. They always argued that, in doing so, they were acting to reinforce the democratic work of Parliament by keeping the executive within the scope of what the judges believed Parliament had intended. Lord Justice Stephen Sedley even spoke of a 'dual sovereignty' between Parliament and the judiciary in keeping the executive accountable.[16] This has included requiring the Thatcher government to hold elections for the Inner

London Education Authority which it had already declared its inten-
tion to abolish, and delaying the introduction of teachers' performance-related pay because Education Secretary David Blunkett had
not consulted Parliament fully.

Supporters of the governments thus affected were predictably
furious, accusing judges of 'playing politics', interfering with the
fulfilment of policy pledges made at elections. 'It is', said Tory MP
David Wilshire, 'high time they came out of their courtrooms and
stood for elections if this is the game they want to play.' His Conservative colleague, Sir Ivan Lawrence QC, MP, told the Commons that
it was 'a great pity that some members of the judiciary go out of the
way to show how out of touch they are with the British people's feelings'. Boris Johnson wrote in *The Spectator* that judges were frustrated
Labour politicians, but the then Shadow Lord Chancellor, Derry
Irvine, was equally fierce in warning judges away from political decision-making. An extended debate took place during the period as to
the extent to which politicians through the Commons should set
minimum sentences for certain offences, and to which the Home
Secretary should intervene to alter sentences according to public petition. This debate has continued under subsequent Home Secretaries,
reflected in the controversy over the sentence of the killers of Jamie
Bulger, and over the increased use of mandatory sentencing.[17] Tony
Blair went as far as to warn judges after the London bombings of July
2005 that the public would not tolerate leniency in the treatment of
suspected terrorists:

> We have tried to get rid of them [suspected terrorists] and have been
> blocked . . . I think there has been too great a caution in saying, 'sorry
> this is unacceptable' . . . The independence of the judiciary is a prin-
> ciple of our democracy and we have to uphold it but I hope that
> recent events have created a situation where people understand that
> it is important that we do protect ourselves.[18]

This leaves a most confused picture for those seeking democracy.
Judges have it as their job not to make democratic policy decisions, but
to maintain the framework within which liberal democracy can successfully operate. Yet they are accused by both Left and Right of going
beyond their proper role, and interfering with the implementation
of mandates or other measures reflecting public opinion. Whether

judges' theoretical role is a democratic one is a reflection of the debate in Part I as to whether civil rights are an inherent part of democracy; the extent to which they have expanded, or exceeded, that role is likewise a matter of dispute, which will be fuelled by Jack Straw's incorporation of the European Convention on Human Rights into English Law. Like civil servants and peers, however, the judges' role is inherently undemocratic – or, at any rate, non-democratic – because they have no relationship other than goodwill with the citizenry. They can only make democracy *possible*; anything they do to make it actually happen is pure accident.

Pluralism

The institutions turned to for additional participation in oiling the wheels of British state institutions are, despite some impressive appearances, not reliable vehicles of democracy either. This can be demonstrated by addressing each of the channels of public opinion mentioned above in turn.

Parties

While it is true that politicians cannot ignore their party, and that parties may express opinions learned from, or shared with, the wider public, the fact is that parties are in decline in respect of all their key democratic functions. Keith Sutherland's recent study made the bold claim that 'the political party is an anachronism. It serves no useful purpose and we are better off without it. Furthermore, it is a danger to democracy and an affront to the constitutional dignity of our country.'[19]

Firstly, political parties are smaller than in the past. Whereas in the 1950s there were over a million individual members of the Labour Party, and around 2.8 million Conservatives, those figures now stand at little more than 300,000 for the Conservatives, and only 214,000 for Labour (despite a brief recovery at the time of the 1997 election). The age of the mass party has undoubtedly passed. Moreover, as was always the case, this dwindling number of supporters is not representative of the public as a whole, either socially or politically. Party members tend to be disproportionately middle class and, in the case of the Conservatives, the most recent comprehensive study also showed that their average age was sixty-three. It is widely thought, for example, that while news of Mrs Thatcher's unpopularity was filtered up through the party in 1990, most Tory members did not wish her to be removed. In the only leadership election in which all members could vote directly, the Conservatives chose the electorally unsuccessful Iain Duncan Smith as their leader in 2001. One of the supporters of his opponent, Kenneth Clarke, went as far as to say that the 300,000 Conservatives were the only group of that number in Britain among whom a majority preferring Iain Duncan Smith could be found. Most even of this unusual selection of citizens are not active in their party, either: Seyd et al. found that 80 per cent of Conservatives took part in party activities less than once a month.[20] Those who are active (and therefore have greater influence upon the party's profile) may hold very different views on some subjects than the remainder of the membership, let alone the wider public. A report in the *Guardian* on 14 April 2000 claimed that one in three Constituency Labour Parties had failed to take up their representation at the coming Labour Conference, and that their seats would be sold instead to corporate sponsors; a week later, a report in *The Times* of the lowest Conservative Party membership figures since World War I prompted a campaigner for greater democracy within the Tory party, John Strafford, to say: 'The Tory and Labour parties are in terminal decline outside Parliament. It is because they are undemocratic. People who join leave when they find they have no power or influence.'

On matters of policy, parties can be equally unrepresentative, or conversely can be marginalised. Hence the Labour Party Conference in the early 1980s adopted a series of radical policies that contributed substantially to the party's massive defeats in 1983 and 1987; the Conservatives, with historically unusual insensitivity, have manifestly failed to strike a chord with enough of the British public to reverse their electoral defeats of 1997, 2001 and 2005. This failure was examined in detail before the 2005 election by Pippa Norris and Joni Lovenduski, who concluded that the Tories suffer from 'Selective Perception':

> The Conservatives face multiple problems – of membership, of organization and of leadership. But this study provides substantial evidence that ideological patterns of party competition have structured and

contributed towards Conservative failure, and Labour success, in the last two elections. The Conservatives lost, not just because of Hague's image, the Millbank machine, or the economy, but also because they did not understand what was necessary in order to win. As in therapy, the first step towards recovery is to recognize a problem. The second is summoning up the will to change. Until these blinkers are stripped, it seems unlikely that the Conservatives will take the first steps towards restoring their electoral fortunes.[21]

These failures to respond to changes in public opinion may, in fact, be the responsibility of the leadership as much as the membership because the party organisations have, at best, only a limited impact upon their leaders. The Labour Party, in particular, has transferred policy-making under Tony Blair away from the Party Conference to policy forums with fewer and more predictable members. The main conference has become in effect a rally for television purposes rather like presidential nomination conventions in the United States. Conference managers were embarrassed in 2004 by publication in the press of instructions circulated among delegates about when and how to give applause to the leader's speech.

Thus, as mechanisms for informing the public or as vehicles of public opinion during parliaments, parties are of limited use. The fact is that, when parties were mass organisations, many of their members joined for reasons of leisure and entertainment which are not applicable in the society of the twenty-first century. There were, for example, hundreds of Labour, Conservative and Liberal social clubs whose doors are now closed; the Young Conservatives alone had a membership of 150,000, and gloried in its reputation – not entirely facetious – as Europe's biggest dating agency. Labour candidate and author, Paul Richards, asked anxiously in a Fabian Society pamphlet of 2000: 'How can political entities founded one hundred or more years ago possibly compete for the attention of a population which is better educated, housed, nourished and entertained than any in history? How can the local party branch meeting or fundraising Summer Ball compete with a trip to the multiplex or a couple of hours of *Tomb Raider*?'[22] The membership of parties never has been a reliably representative sample of the public, nor has it necessarily been ideologically coherent but, today, it is a particularly odd place to look for a democratic mandate.

Box 5.2 Declining party membership in the United Kingdom

Source A: Membership of the Conservative and Labour Parties, 1953–2003 (figures in millions)

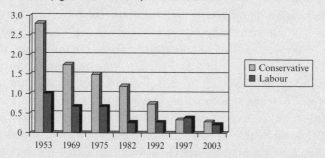

Source B: from Mike Rowe, 'Is the Party Over for Political Parties?', Politics Review, *September 2002*

'The parties themselves see their members as a source of legitimacy: the members represent the aspirations of a large proportion of society. It may have been for this reason that Tony Blair's reinvention of the Labour Party included a pledge to recruit a million members. There was some initial success on this front, but in 1998 and again in 2002 membership levels fell significantly. The data presented here suggest that membership of the major political parties in the UK is low by EU standards and is declining, but this decline reflects a general trend . . . Party membership represents less than 2% of the total UK electorate; only France has a lower percentage. However, with the clear exceptions of Austria and Finland, the party membership figure does not rise above 7% for the other member states of the EU . . . Party membership is in decline in most EU countries, although Spain, Greece and Portugal clearly buck this trend. The UK fares relatively badly, with a decline in party membership of more than 50% in the 20 years to 2000. Whether this represents a disillusionment with the political process or the fickleness of individuals in terms of party loyalty, or some combination of the two, is open to debate.'

Why are British voters no longer prepared to join major political parties?

Pressure groups

It is certainly true that 'cause' pressure groups have grown in size and public recognition in the last twenty years. To credit such pressure groups with revitalising democracy, however, is to confuse visibility with both popularity and power.

Until the 1980s, democracy was thought well served by corporatism, that is, the direct negotiation of government policies with sizeable and strategically important pressure groups, notably the Confederation of British Industry and the Trade Union Congress. This left parliamentarians feeling out in the cold: even supporters of the governments concerned complained of being 'kept in ignorance of the "horse-trading" of interest groups'. Unaccountable and unrepresentative factions were, it was argued, being given more control over public policy than democratically elected members of Parliament. With the Thatcher governments, however, formalised arrangements over pay, prices and social policy, such as the 'Social Contract' of the mid-1970s, were abandoned in favour of a more *ad hoc* relationship with pressure groups, who entered into a sort of free-market competition for the attention of government. From this, some groups benefited more than others: think-tanks, such as the Adam Smith Institute, gained prominence; the Institute of Directors began to displace the CBI as the government's contact with business; and 'cause' groups, notably environmental ones such as Friends of the Earth, grew in membership and publicity, sometimes by taking direct action. A critical view might be that the pressure groups which became 'insiders' during this period were the ones telling governments what they wanted to hear. This apparently more flexible pressure-group system was regarded by some as a valuable expression of public opinion where Parliament and the parties had failed; but this is arguable.

Firstly, it is wrong to suppose that the most visible pressure groups are the most influential ones. This was best illustrated by the controversy surrounding the exemption by Tessa Jowell, junior public health minister, of Formula One racing from the ban on sponsorship by tobacco companies which was imposed upon all other sports in November 1997. It emerged that Bernie Ecclestone, President of the Formula One Association, had donated £1 million to the Labour Party's election coffers. The following July, a lobbyist and former adviser to Peter Mandelson, Derek Draper, was revealed as having told clients of his firm that, for a fee, he could put them in contact with the 'seventeen people who count' (most of them not ministers) in the government. In many ways, the resort to public protests by organisations such as Greenpeace is a sign of their failure to influence the government by less inconvenient methods, albeit their strategy may produce some results in the long run. This is especially clearly demonstrated by the tactical development of the Countryside Alliance, whose supporters became less reluctant to use illegal and even violent methods, including clashes with the police in Parliament Square and breaking on to the floor of the Commons in November 2004, as their cause moved closer and closer to legislative defeat.

Secondly, the success of a group (or its visibility) is not necessarily linked to its size, nor to its expression of wider public opinion. Larger groups in Britain, such as trade unions like Unison (1,272,000 members) and the Transport and General Workers Union (881,000), or environmental groups, such as Greenpeace (169,000) or the Ramblers' Association (128,000), have enjoyed varying levels of impact on government policy over time. This has depended heavily upon their resources – the Greenpeace occupation of the Brent Spar oil platform in 1995, for example, cost the group £350,000 for the equipment to televise the event; the effectiveness of their network of contacts with local authorities, central government, European institutions, the media and others; the effectiveness of their organisation and leadership; and the strategic importance of direct action (such as striking) they might take. Martin J. Smith's recent analysis concluded that it is 'extremely difficult to make generalisations about the power of pressure groups', but that, contrary to Punnett, 'government can survive without pressure groups but pressure groups cannot survive without government'.[23]

Whatever the cocktail of circumstances which gives a pressure group influence, it has little to do with democracy, for we have little way of knowing which groups represent public opinion, or even represent their own 'armchair' membership authentically. For all the publicity they received, why are we to presume that the protesters against the Newbury bypass in 1996 had any more of a mandate than the local council, local MP and the national government, all of whom favoured the development? To take a challenging recent case, the controversy over fox-hunting ranged the newly formed Countryside Alliance, capable of organising annual protests of over 100,000 people (and with close contacts in the Conservative leadership) against the Ramblers' Association, the League Against Cruel Sports and the vast majority of MPs in a series of free votes. Which of these represents public opinion? Polls would appear to indicate the latter organisations, but they also seem to show that the public does not see this, nor animal welfare generally, as a key issue, despite the high profile it has received in the media. Of course, we would not wish democracy to be judged entirely by opinion polls but then we do not know how many of those on the Countryside Alliance marches were principally concerned with the distinctive issue of fox-hunting.

Recent examples of high-profile pressure-group activity have illustrated this democratic ambiguity further. The fuel protestors of autumn 2000, who blockaded refineries and caused petrol shortages, seemed to enjoy some public sympathy and, indeed, their activities coincided with the only poll findings of that Parliament in which the Conservatives matched Labour; but, later in the year, public sympathy died away with the second protest which enjoyed far less favourable media coverage than the first campaign. Tony Blair dismissed the blockades as undemocratic, using public suffering to try to force the government's hand; and yet, in subsequent budgets, Gordon Brown sought to ease the burden of tax on petrol. Though also condemned by the government for its strike action in 2003, the Fire Brigades Union secured a substantial pay rise – substantial, as least, when compared with those granted to members of public-sector unions that declined to strike, such as the Royal College of Nursing. The 'Stop the War' Coalition seemed to enjoy substantial support, and raised a million-strong demonstration in London in February 2003, but was ignored by the government; whereas 'Fathers 4 Justice', a tiny group aiming to improve the legal position of divorced fathers denied access to their children, achieved front-page publicity on every national newspaper after climbing the walls of Buckingham Palace in 2004, and, within days, there had been promises of a review of family law from the Home Secretary and from his Shadow. Most recently, the Live 8 campaign to urge G8 ministers meeting at Gleneagles to take action against Third World poverty was declared by its leader, Bob Geldof, to have been an unqualified success; yet this was possible because the exact aims even of the campaign – let alone its supporters – had remained vague. The campaign's publicity had owed more to the celebrity of its leaders than to the force of its arguments or even to the numbers of its followers.

This raises another important problem about pressure groups, associated with Michels's 'Iron law of oligarchy'. Not only is the success of a pressure group not related to its closeness to public opinion, but it is doubtful whether groups' leaders are always representative even of their own members. Who can say what the demands and priorities of the millions of supporters of loose networks, such as Stop the War, Live 8 or the fuel protestors? Even more established and formal organisations can experience such a disjuncture: Andy Gilchrist, leader of the Fire Brigades Union, found himself replaced as leader in 2005 because of his members' resentment of his handling of the dispute two years earlier. Thus, pressure groups may have little claim to a public mandate, and only a fragile claim to one from their own membership, especially if it is large and fluid. Those that are successful may not be those that have a better claim on these two fronts, but which are blessed with good political contacts, plentiful resources, favourable relations with the media and the ability to do damage if snubbed. This hardly seems a recipe for democracy. Even a sympathetic observer of pressure groups, such as Wyn Grant, who concludes that 'pressure groups do make a significant contribution to democracy', acknowledges that the limits upon the pressure group system are its tendency to reflect existing inequalities of power:

> Although class analysis is no longer popular, the pressure group world is inhabited largely by members of the middle class or at least the highly educated. As Schatterschneider observed, 'The flaw in the pluralist heaven is that the heavenly chorus sings with a strong upper-class accent.' Perhaps the accent is estuarine English rather than upper class these days, but the voices are generally those of the included rather than the excluded.[24]

Lastly, popular or not, pressure groups do sometimes simply make mistakes. Especially under the stress of the need to win publicity, it is tempting for activists to exaggerate their case, or to neglect evidence contrary to it. The battle between Shell UK and Greenpeace over the company's plans to dump the Brent Spar oil installation in the North Sea ended ironically after an international boycott organised by the environmentalists convinced the company to abandon the plan in June 1995. It later emerged, however, that the toxic impact of the dumping of the rig would have been far less than Greenpeace had anticipated. Even as informers of public debate, pressure groups can be counter-productive.

Media

Whether as conveyors of information to the public, or as of public opinion to the government, the media's role is equivocal. Certainly it is true that Prime Ministers pursue press proprietors (as Blair has with Rupert Murdoch) and that their press secretaries alternately cultivate and intimidate journalists. Indeed, ministers are often accused by MPs, such as Clare Short in her 2003 resignation statement to the Commons, of being obsessed with public relations and the effect of 'spin doctoring'. This does not, however, denote the fulfilment of a democratic function on the part of the press or broadcasters.

A three-way relationship may be said to exist between the media, the public and the government. In a democratic state of affairs, the relationship would consist of a collaboration between the public and the media, with the former as the senior partner, to investigate and determine how the government behaves. The relationship may be one, however, in which the media are implored by politicians to pressurise the public, as in the quadrille danced by Blair, Major and (on Major's behalf, but apparently to Blair's benefit) Margaret Thatcher around Murdoch in the run-up to 1997. There may be an attempt by the media to rouse the public against the government, as occurred from 1993 onwards when the Eurosceptic right-wing press turned on Major after the Maastricht Treaty, and (in the case of the *Daily Mail* and some coverage in the *Sun*) even supported the implausible challenge of John Redwood to the Tory leader in 1995. The public, the media and politicians all have their own agendas – and, of course, each of those three encompasses a huge variety of different agendas that are often contradictory to one another.

During the 1980s and early 1990s, it was widely believed that the preference of the media for the Conservatives – 80 per cent of newspaper circulation was pro-Tory – and the particularly unashamed vilification in some quarters of Neil Kinnock had cost Labour the 1992 election. One estimate argued that public opinion had been moved 1 per cent in the Conservatives' favour by press coverage at each election since the 1950s; research by *Guardian* journalist, Martin Linton, supported Neil Kinnock's acknowledgement of the *Sun*'s boast that 'It's

The Sun Wot Won It' immediately after Major's victory. Certainly, the weight of newspaper bias did not reflect the more balanced picture of public opinion, although it may have altered it.

As to investigating government and informing the public, the deterioration in the seriousness of tabloid coverage has compromised this function considerably. To compete with television, reporting has in all titles become ever more brief and sensational, and television has repaid the compliment, with ever shorter news bulletins, of which Channel Five's and BBC Three's are perhaps the best (or worst) examples. Franklin described the deterioration of news media values into entertainment values in *Newszak and News Media* in 1997.[25] Reporters remain reliant upon the co-operation of politicians for much of their work, as was demonstrated by the failure of broadcasters to arrange debates between the party leaders in the last three general elections, and as is proving true even in the passage of the Freedom of Information Act, into which ministers have inserted exemptions covering concealment of advice they receive from civil servants. Downing Street continues to give favour to those journalists who use early hints of prime ministerial intentions favourably, and punishes the critical journalist. The **news management** process of the Labour leadership was perhaps most notoriously exposed with the revelation that Jo Moore, special adviser to Transport Secretary. Stephen Byers, had sent a message to colleagues on hearing about the tragic news of 11 September 2001, saying that it would be 'a very good day to get out anything we want to bury', but is personified by the pro-active and highly partisan image of Alastair Campbell as the Prime Minister's Press Secretary.

The media sometimes help to inform and give voice to the public. Yet, in doing so, like the parties and pressure groups, it competes with Parliament as the source of democratic legitimacy. Speaker Boothroyd complained in April 2000 that ministers were announcing policy proposals on television and radio without putting them before Parliament for scrutiny, and that 'the interests of Parliament are regarded as secondary to media presentation'. Worse still, the media may hold up a distorting mirror to public opinion, and one which the public itself begins to accept. More importantly for democracy, the media's role is distorted firstly by their own agenda, and secondly by that of the government upon which they depend for information. Neither of these can be identified systematically with the public will.

. . . .

☑ What you should have learnt from reading this chapter

This chapter has touched upon some important criticisms of the Westminster model as a realistic conception of democracy in modern Britain. The criticisms come from Conservative, Liberal, Socialist and other traditions, and are often not consistent, and imply very varied solutions. The reasons that the Westminster model fails – to the extent that it does – might be placed under at least three main headings:

- Elements of the system do not seek to be purely democratic. Some pressure-group activity, some media campaigns, and clearly the work of the Lords, the Civil Service and the courts are intended at their most democratic to preserve the 'liberal' elements of liberal democracy, that is, the rights or claims of a minority against or to the public at large. They might more bluntly be described as defending established interests or a presumption of greater insight against clearly expressed public opinion. To the extent that these conflicts arise, they reflect the tensions inherent in liberal or conservative conceptions of democracy.

- Some elements reflect the difficulty in determining what the democratic mandate is: the problems of interpreting election results; or of assessing the level of popular sympathy for pressure groups or media campaigns, are evidence that public opinion is impossible to pin down. This reflects the problem of identifying and acting upon the General Will. Even if we wanted to do as the public directed, we would have to work out what it was first. As outgoing American President Bill Clinton said wryly amid confusion about the outcome of the contest to be his predecessor in November 2000: 'The people have spoken; but nobody is quite sure what they said.'

- Some problems arise from change in British society. Criticism of the British system of government has grown since the 1960s for a variety of reasons: the disappointing economic performance of governments, the spread of broadcasting and other forms of political communication, the increasing diversity of identities among the British public, and the decline of mass institutions and interests, such as manufacturing industry and trade unions, have all contributed to alienation on the part of elements of the electorate, and the search for alternative ways of gaining access to power.

What this reminds us of is the fact that democracy cannot simply be measured by the existence of institutions (since these have remained in place throughout the process of that alienation); rather it is reflected in the relationship between those institutions and the social context in which they operate, as well as the expectations made of the system. The Westminster system, it is probably fair to say, reflects public opinion less successfully in a multi-party, regionally fragmented, culturally diverse and economically less secure and stable society than in the one of the 1950s. The nature of the criticisms is also significant, because they are themselves diverse and in some ways contradictory. Needless to say, all of the above assumes that the system either did once work, or was intended to work. Even assuming this, once the process of decline was underway, interests rather than principles would certainly begin to prevail. Evidently, to gain general agreement about the weaknesses of a system is difficult enough; finding remedies agreed by all those dissatisfied is doubly hard.

Glossary of key terms

British presidency Phrase used by Michael Foley among others to describe the way in which the power and authority of the Prime Minister no longer come from a relationship with the Cabinet and Parliament, but rather with the public as a whole, largely via the media.

Democratic deficit The difference between public opinion and the policy implemented by government. This is most often applied to the UK's relationship with Europe, but is also used in discussion of Parliament, the electoral system and other features of the Westminster model.

Dominant-party system A relationship between major parties in which only one has any realistic prospect of winning elections, leading to a concentration of debate within that party, and disillusionment within others.

Elective Dictatorship The phrase used by Lord Hailsham to describe the enormous powers possessed by the executive once supported by a majority in the Commons. This stresses the limits upon the constraints offered by parties, Parliament, the courts, the press or local government.

News management The manipulation of information available to, and used by, the media so as to create a favourable impression of, say, the government. This might involve announcing policies twice, 'covering' bad news with other stories, or withholding information from critical journalists.

Likely examination questions

How much control does Parliament exercise over the executive?

What criticisms have been made of elections to the House of Commons?

Why do parties fail to convey public opinion successfully?

In what ways is the Westminster model a dangerous myth?

Helpful websites

These sites, both run by university politics departments, are not in themselves relentlessly critical of the Constitution, but they provide useful up-to-date audits of the state of British democracy, and **some** analysis that may provoke doubts about the effectiveness of our institutions:

www.revolts.co.uk

www.ucl.ac.uk/constitution-unit/index.php

These two are the sites of organisations critical of the current system of government:

www.makemyvotecount.org.uk/news.html

www.charter88.org.uk/

Suggestions for further reading

The first two titles here are recent academic critical surveys of the institutions and processes of British democracy, the third focuses on the role of Parliament:

Peter Hennessy, *The Hidden Wiring: Unearthing the British Constitution* (Victor Gollancz, 1995).

G. Parry, G. Moyser and N. Day, *Political Participation and Democracy in Britain* (Cambridge University Press, 1992).

Peter Riddell, *Parliament Under Blair* (Politico's, 1998).

The following are from three journalists, all offering critical judgements on British democracy. The last is broadly of the Left; the first and second right wing.

Simon Jenkins, *Accountable to None* (Penguin, 1996).

Andrew Marr, *Ruling Britannia: The Failure and Future of British Democracy* (Michael Joseph, 1995).

Ferdinand Mount, *The British Constitution Now* (Mandarin, 1993).

The Remedies

Contents

Overview

The Labour Party came into government in 1997 carried forward by much of the criticism of the British system of government explained in Chapter 5. Its programme – described by more than one of its supporters as 'revolutionary', and condemned by the Conservatives as destructive of all that is good about British democracy – included the most sweeping set of promises of constitutional reform in any Labour manifesto: reform of the Lords and of local government; introduction of devolution and electoral reform; and the ending of government secrecy were only the main items. Tony Blair claimed that it was 'the biggest programme of change to democracy ever proposed'. Chapter 6 examines some of these changes, and other possible reforms, to ask what the route to a more democratic Britain might look like – and whether we might want to travel it.

Key issues to be covered in this chapter

- What changes to the British system of government have been proposed and implemented recently?
- Who has made these proposals?
- Who has opposed them?
- To what extent would their implementation enhance British democracy?
- Is that always desirable?

The electoral system

The debate about whether the first-past-the-post system is more or less democratic than any of the alternatives is a familiar and extensive one, a full treatment of which is not possible here. The central issue is that of whether the government formed following an election under any system has a mandate to conduct itself in office, the contention of electoral reformers being that single-party governments endorsed by only a minority of the national vote do not.

It is by no means clear, however, that coalition governments constructed from parties whose combined vote exceeds 50 per cent of the total are in any better moral position. For, while the Blair government was at least identifiably chosen by 44 per cent of those voting on 1 May 1997, a government made up of Labour and Liberal Democrat ministers (the most likely outcome under any other system) was chosen by nobody, and its policies would have reflected the need to maintain the support of that group of MPs elected by the smallest number of voters, namely the Liberal Democrats. The logic of proportional representation presumes that votes are cast for party labels, and that the mandates of parties can be stitched together without compromising the integrity of each respective party.

The first of these propositions, as we have seen, is doubtful indeed, at least as a complete explanation of voting; the second is impossible to prove. In fact, the outcomes of coalition bargains depend more upon the short- and medium-term objectives of the politicians involved than upon the reflection of the public will at any given time. Of course, it would be folly for any party openly to defy its own voters or potential voters in the terms it agreed to in coalition; a given party's voters may be only a small minority of the electorate, however, beyond which it feels no pressing need to extend its support. The modification of Labour's commitment to higher education tuition fees in Scotland, and the removal of Alun Michael as First Secretary in Wales, were the results of circumstances created by the use of proportional representation but, whether or not these changes reflected public opinion in the two countries, that was not the reason directly which caused them to take place. The introduction of proportional representation to Scottish local government as part of the second Scottish executive's package of policies takes this a step further: its popularity with voters is less clear than was the ending of tuition fees, it clearly serves the interests of some parties more than others, and it extends the prospect of further negotiation across the Scottish political system.

At local level, the choice given to voters over candidates can be markedly reduced under proportional representation, especially under those systems that entail party lists, such as were used in the European Assembly elections in June 1999, and in the 'top-up' elements of the Welsh Assembly and Scottish Parliament. In these systems, party officials have far greater influence over who becomes a candidate in a given area, and this meant that some figures, such as Labour left-wing MP Denis Canavan, were excluded from the party's list for the first Scottish Parliament (although he was subsequently elected as a first-past-the-post member on an independent ticket).

Few would argue that electoral reform has caused or would cause widespread confusion, but neither has it raised turnout or improved public faith in the institutions thus elected. That seems to depend upon a much wider context of perception of 'delivery' by the institutions and conduct of their personnel. As the dust settles on the use of new electoral systems, it begins to look as though neither the hopes nor the fears raised by them have been fully realised.

Parliament

The Labour government of 1997 established a select committee of MPs to examine the Commons' operation and to recommend changes. More attention has been directed, however, at changes in the composition of the Lords.

The so-called **Modernisation** Committee was established under the aegis of Leader of the House, Ann Taylor, with the purpose of examining procedures in Parliament and eliminating unnecessary obstacles to MPs' work. Within a year it had issued three reports, but had made very few changes in parliamentary practice, partly because of resistance from Number 10 Downing Street and partly because of Taylor's determination to make any reforms the product of cross-party consensus. The reports made useful minor suggestions, such as removing the priority given to privy councillors to speak in debates, but rejected more substantial changes such as electronic voting in the chamber or even allowing MPs to applaud in the Commons. The committee's proposals have been just that and, while limited alterations have been made to the Commons timetable (such as moving to one thirty-minute Prime Minister's questions slot), these have been neither root and branch nor unequivocally directed at strengthening the position of MPs *vis-à-vis* the executive. Indeed, the reduction of the number of Prime Minister's questions sessions has come under some criticism in a context in which Tony Blair attends only 5 per cent of parliamentary divisions. It is the power of the executive, exercised through the whips and the patronage of the Prime Minister, that has to be restrained, perhaps by the election of select committee members, or even of the Cabinet. Neither of these seems likely.

In the Lords, however, dramatic and visible changes have occurred, although they have scarcely rendered the legislature more democratic. The centuries-old controversy of whether or not Parliament should include persons who gain their places there by birth has been largely (though not entirely) resolved by the reduction of the number of hereditary peers from over 750 to ninety-two, elected by the former number. This is the first stage of a two-part process, the second stage of which will involve a restructuring of the whole membership of the Lords. A Royal Commission on the Lords was appointed by Tony Blair in 1999 under Conservative former cabinet minister, Lord Wakeham, to explore the possible alternatives, and its report later in the year suggested a house composed of a mixture of appointed and elected members.[1] The Wakeham proposals, and others by Lord Irvine, were abandoned in the face of opposition at Westminster. Attempts to resolve this situation came to a head in February 2003, when MPs held a series of free votes on four options, ranging from a wholly appointed second chamber (the Prime Minister's preferred option) to a wholly elected one. All four options were defeated (though in the case of the 80 per cent elected, 20 per cent appointed option, it was by only three votes). This stalemate reflects the difficulty in resolving the dilemma of recognising undemocratic authority in a supposedly democratic constitution.

The government claimed that the hereditary peers caused a 'lack of legitimacy' in the Lords because of their consistent preference for the Conservatives, even in the face of Labour election victories. Certainly, it is true that, from the 1960s to the 1990s, Labour governments were defeated on average forty-two times a year by the Lords, whereas the average for Conservative administrations was only twelve. At the time of their removal, 304 of the hereditaries were Conservatives, while only forty-two were Labour or Liberal Democrat. Their removal would appear to be a democratic measure, therefore, allowing the democratic mandate of Labour governments to be put into effect.

As with other British institutions, however, these reforms will end valuable non-democratic functions performed by the Lords, while introducing a new system of dubious democratic credentials, or one in which its democracy creates new problems. Following the growth in numbers of life peers since 1958, the 'professionalism' (that is, attendance at, and quality of, debates and questions) of the upper house has increased markedly. It passes more legislation than most elected chambers around the world, and brings to bear upon it the weight of experience and expertise of former cabinet ministers, civil servants, academics, scientists, journalists, trade unionists, business people, local government officers, film directors and all the other figures who have been awarded places in the Lords. The Lords' legitimacy arises not from election, but from knowledge (a source of authority acknowledged to some extent by most liberal and conservative writers introduced in Part I), and any move towards a more democratic chamber will necessarily compromise that legitimacy. The second chamber may still perform a useful function, but it will not be the one of reviewing legislation from the vantage point of experience.

More fundamental than the problems of losing the authority of experience are the problems of claiming democratic credentials. An elected second chamber will either duplicate the first, which would be needless, or challenge it, which would be potentially chaotic. An upper house elected by proportional representation, for example, might well feel itself entitled to veto legislation proposed by a less representative (as peers would see it) Commons; at the very least, the new house would be much more likely to use its delaying powers to the full on a regular basis.

The central problem of Parliament's democratic legitimacy cannot be resolved by procedural or even structural reforms: it is the question of where the mandate lies. MPs claim a right to act and vote as individual constituency representatives; whips assert that MPs were elected only as party candidates; and pressure groups, the media and other interests demand that Parliament's authority rests partly upon its willingness to respond to them. Altering the parliamentary timetable does nothing to adjudicate between these claims; replacing the Lords with an elected chamber merely creates another arena in which these rival forces can argue their cases, while losing the benefits of a house less vulnerable to the whips, pressure groups and short-term movements in public opinion. This is not to say that none of these solutions is satisfactory; but equally, none is ideally democratic, and none is cost free.

The Prime Minister

Critiques of the growth of prime ministerial power are far thicker on the ground than proposals for resolving the problems it creates. One example is the constitutional reform package proposed by veteran Labour MP and former cabinet minister, Tony Benn, in *Arguments for Democracy* (1981) and in the 1990s in his Commonwealth of Britain Bill. Benn proposes turning the 'Absolute Premiership' we have into a 'Constitutional' one by divesting the Prime Minister of certain central powers. He argues for the election of the Cabinet (and confirmation of their portfolios) by all MPs of the ruling group; curtailment of prime ministerial patronage by ending peerages, and introducing a system of parliamentary control over public appointments to bodies such as Royal Commissions; and the publication of cabinet minutes.[2]

These measures would, in some important ways, strengthen Parliament's (and the Cabinet's) hand against the Prime Minister although it is interesting to note that Benn is one of those most keen to make MPs accountable to their extra-parliamentary party, too, and this might cause its own difficulties (see below). The weaknesses of these proposals are, as with others, twofold: that they might destabilise accountable government; or that they might not make much difference at all. The election of cabinet members and the publication of minutes of their discussions would increase divisions within the Cabinet, and thereby be likely to compromise collective responsibility (as Benn fully intends it should). It could, therefore, actually be harder for the Commons to hold ministers accountable, as they would endeavour to disown policies that proved ineffective or unpopular.

More likely, however, is the prospect that these mechanisms would not diminish the power of the Prime Minister, because the full Cabinet has relatively little impact upon policy making. As at present, Prime Ministers would be able to resolve most important issues in informal meetings with sympathetic ministers, cabinet committees, or by agreement of his 'inner' cabinet of trusted and loyal colleagues. Even given the chance to elect the Cabinet, back-benchers would be restrained by the knowledge that the personality and strategy of the leader made certain choices of minister especially controversial and divisive.

Recently, some proponents of parliamentary reform have argued that the changed role of the Prime Minister into that of an effective president should be recognised: Graham Allen MP has suggested that the premier be elected independently of Parliament, as is now the system in towns and cities that have directly elected mayors. Allen acknowledges that 'a whole set of new working relationships with Parliament and the Executive would be necessary so that business could be dealt with expeditiously'.[3] If Foley's analysis of the Prime Minister's role is correct, however, this might be only a recognition and accountability of a position the PM already holds. To assess this, we need to look at elected mayors and, of course, at the independently elected presidents abroad to see if they seem to fulfil our idea of democracy better than the present arrangements.

Some efforts have been made by Tony Blair to modernise the premiership, such as inviting film-maker Michael Cockerell to document the role of Alastair Campbell as the PM's Press Secretary, and holding regular press conferences; but most of these have been criticised as increasing the power of the Prime Minister, whose power is reflected in procedures, but emanates from relationships with the media, the parties, Parliament and international organisations, none of which is easily controlled. Denis Kavanagh commented early in Blair's premiership that 'Blair's efforts to reshape the British Premiership have certainly been radical', but that 'Blair, for all his interest in **devolution**, has been a centraliser in party management and in running the machinery of government'.[4]

The parties

Since in mass representative democracies, parties are an almost inevitable feature of elections and parliaments, they may be regarded as a promising means of controlling the actions of politicians between elections and the promises they make in campaigns. It was this hope that gave birth to the 'Charter' movement in the Conservative Party, and the Campaign for Labour Party Democracy (CLPD), in the 1970s, following each main party's decline in membership and support at the polls. Each of these campaigns argued that, by giving greater control over policies, MPs, and the leader to members of their party outside Parliament, they could revive public faith both in that party and in democratic government itself. Many of their demands have been met, but the outcome has been less dramatic than was hoped.

The defeat of the Labour Party in 1979 was attributed by many of its members to the failure of the Callaghan government to fulfil election promises or to adhere to conference decisions on matters such as pay policy, abolition of the Lords and nationalisation. To bind the parliamentary leadership to wider opinion, the CLPD campaigned for the introduction of an electoral college reflecting all elements of the party to choose future leaders, rather than just the MPs (as it had been to that point); the mandatory reselection of MPs by their constituency parties; and the power of veto over manifesto contents to be given to the National Executive Committee, elected by the party conference.

While there have been fierce arguments about the conduct of the elections within the Labour Party (particularly about whether organisations within the party, such as unions, should vote as blocks or by 'one member one vote'), the basic argument for participation by members outside Parliament has been won convincingly. Tony Blair was elected Labour leader in 1994 by an electoral college giving equal say to MPs and MEPs, trade unions and constituency parties respectively, and in which most of those bodies gave individual votes to their members. This meant that some 952,000 people participated directly in the vote. In 1996 Labour adopted the novel practice of sending its draft manifesto to all 377,000 party members for approval or rejection: 95 per cent of those replying (in a 61 per cent turnout) approved it.

The Conservatives' 1997 manifesto was constructed through a less systematic and compelling, but widespread, process of formal consultation meetings which followed a promise made in the 1995 leadership contest. The Tories first turned to balloting members when William Hague consolidated his policy of opposition to British membership of the European single currency for at least ten years by a vote of Conservative members, 80 per cent of whom backed him in a postal ballot in 1998. This followed Hague's confirmation of a new two-stage electoral system for the Conservative leadership in which a vote among MPs would reduce the field to two candidates, between whom a run-off would take place in a ballot of all members.

This, and the apparently increasing willingness of local branches of both parties to issue demands to their MPs (for instance to Tim Yeo that he resign as a government minister in January 1995) and in rare cases deselect them, suggest that parties are active and powerful vehicles of popular opinion. Yet this superficial impression is mistaken: first of all, as was observed earlier, the opinions of party members do not necessarily reflect those of the wider public. Some traditionalists have also worried that party members do not know enough about the talents and records of the candidates in leadership elections to make meaningful decisions, and that parliamentary sovereignty may be undermined by the ruling party being saddled with a leader held in contempt by most of his or her MPs. It was for this reason that former Labour MP and television journalist, Brian Walden, described the electoral college as 'the stupidest and potentially most dangerous change the Labour Party ever made';[5] 1922 Committee Chairman, Archie Hamilton, used the same argument to resist activist control over the Tory leadership at their 1997 conference.

More importantly, however, the value of a vote is determined by the circumstances in which it is exercised, and these are rarely conducive to membership influence. Blair and Hague left their respective memberships with an effective *fait accompli* in the policy ballots of 1996 and 1998, because they had tied their own leadership, party unity and electoral fortunes to a 'Yes' vote. In leadership elections, members are left at the mercy of their chief source of information, the media: it is noticeable that the two leaders of the three main parties elected by party-wide ballots are somewhat more familiar to television viewers – perhaps more telegenic – than their own party rivals in the contest, and their Conservative opposite number. In some ways, the 'opening up' of leadership choice has, as in the system of primary elections in America, tended to make challenges to party establishments a more cumbersome and expensive process than before. It certainly has not improved the unity or appeal of the parties, since those defeated in the policy polls, such as Michael Heseltine, declared them 'an irrelevance' and referred back to their own mandates as MPs; meanwhile membership of both main parties has slumped since the general election.

The Conservatives' experience since 1997 has been instructive to those who seek to use parties as mechanisms for extending democracy. Having decided in 1998 to elect their leader in any future leadership contest by a run-off between the two leading contenders settled by postal ballot of all 300,000 Conservative members, this system was used for the first time in 2001 to choose Iain Duncan Smith in preference to Kenneth Clarke. Smith, however, was forced to resign two years later following a disappointing lack of progress in the polls. Such was the desire among Conservatives to avoid a repeat of the previous contest that Smith's successor, Michael Howard, took office unopposed, and proposals to put his election to approval by the party membership were quietly dropped. Upon Howard's resignation after the 2005 election, the Conservatives reviewed their leadership election procedure and, at the time of writing, MPs had just proposed to remove entirely the party membership's role in the election.

The fundamental problem is that parties have many functions other than voicing public opinion: they must provide choice at elections, and therefore present distinctive (and sometimes minority) positions; they must campaign in a united and effective fashion; and they must formulate new policies. Not all of these are consistent with acting as a polling organisation. As even sympathetic observers of party democracy, such as Alan Ware, have concluded, 'for democrats, parties remain a source of frustration because they seem so central to the creation of more democratic societies, and yet devising suitable structures for realising this objective seems elusive'.[6]

Referendums

It is often suggested that democracy can be enhanced by the use of referendums to supplement the elections that choose parliaments or local assemblies. Brian Beedham wrote in *The Economist* on the collapse of the Eastern Bloc that liberal democracies such as Britain had no cause for complacency or triumphalism: 'In most places where it is practised . . . democracy is in a condition of arrested development . . . In crude terms, [the] overdue change is a shift from "representative democracy" to "direct democracy" '.[7]

Box 6.1 Problems with reform

What further reforms, if any, would help British democracy?

Source A: Simon Henig, The Second Elections in Scotland and Wales: Issues and Verdicts, *The Federal Union, May 2003*
'A general opinion has developed about devolution in Scotland and Wales. However much dissatisfaction may have been expressed from time to time with the respective performances of the Scottish and Welsh devolved institutions, there was no suggestion in any quarter that the clock should simply be turned back. The concept of devolution has clearly become an accepted part of the political culture in both countries. Put in slightly crude terms there is an unspoken declaration in both Scotland and Wales – "whatever the faults, it is *our* parliament/assembly". Of the major parties, only the SNP fought the elections on a manifesto for major constitutional change. Labour and the Greens in both countries and the Liberal Democrats in Scotland can be classified as "status quo" parties – seemingly broadly content with current institutional arrangements.'

Source B: Mark Rathbone, 'The November 2004 Referendum in the North-East', Talking Politics, *January 2005*
'The fact that there was a gap of six-and-a-half years after 1998 before another referendum was held (apart from small-scale local referendums) makes the device seem less of a permanent feature of the constitution than had been expected in 1998. Although Mitchell and Seyd argued that "it is unlikely that further constitutional reforms will be sufficiently radical to merit similar recourse to a referendum (the possible exception being proposals to radically reform the House of Lords)", it was widely expected in the late 1990s that referendums on the single currency and possibly on electoral reform would be held during the 2001–05 parliament. For a variety of reasons, neither has happened. The government's defeat in the North-East referendum makes it unlikely that the referendums on regional assemblies for Yorkshire and the North-West will ever happen. If past form is any guide, the election of a Conservative Government in 2005 would make the likelihood of any referendums being held in the near future even more remote than if Labour is returned to power.'

Source C: Letter to Labour candidates from Tony Robinson on behalf of Charter 88's 'Elect the Lords' campaign, 15 April 2005
'As you know, the Labour manifesto was published on Wednesday. In it, we commit ourselves to holding a free vote on the composition of the Upper House. This offers us an excellent opportunity to, once

and for all, resolve the issue of Lords reform that has been a thorn in our side since the removal of most of the hereditaries in 1999. But it does mean that, as a candidate, the public has a right to know how you intend to vote in that unwhipped vote.

'One thing is for sure: we can't have a repeat performance of the disastrous series of votes on Lords reform in February 2003 where all the options were defeated. Of the options voted on in the House of Commons, the one that came closest was the 80% elected one – it fell by just 3 votes. A clear majority of MPs – 332 out of 659 – voted for at least one of the 60%, 80% and 100% elected options. And democratic Lords reform is popular: two-thirds of the public support replacing the Lords with a predominantly or wholly elected second chamber.

'So the consensus is for a predominantly elected second chamber. If you are elected next month, you will play a decisive role in determining whether an elected Second Chamber becomes a reality.'

Source D: The Independent, *30 June 2005*
'Tony Blair faced demands from senior MPs yesterday to open up a review of the voting system to give the public a direct say on electoral reform. Robin Cook, the former foreign secretary and leader of the House of Commons, called on Mr Blair to extend a review being conducted by civil servants to the whole country to enable a debate to take place on introducing PR.

'Speaking at a debate on electoral reform, hosted by *The Independent*, Mr Cook made an impassioned plea for a national consultation on the future of the voting system after the Government was elected with only 35 per cent of the vote. The former cabinet minister said voters had a right to contribute to a review on how MPs are chosen and it was wrong to conduct the review behind closed doors. Mr Cook called on the public to "demand . . . that that review is opened up" and "made more transparent". He said the review should "take evidence and meet in public" and "publish its reports so that the people who are involved in choosing the House of Commons are people who themselves have a say in this review and the way in which it [the Commons] is elected." Following the review by the Department for Constitutional Affairs officials, it will be considered by a cabinet committee chaired by John Prescott, the Deputy Prime Minister, who has made clear his opposition for PR for Westminster.
'The debate held last night is part of *The Independent*'s Campaign for Democracy which has now gained the support of 40,000 people or one in six *Independent* readers. Simon Kelner, the Editor in Chief of *The Independent*, who chaired the debate, said the huge degree

of public support for the campaign "gives the lie to the assertion that there isn't any appetite for voting reform".'

Source E: Electoral Commission press release, 19 October 2005
'Take-up of postal voting, at 12.1% of the UK electorate, was three times higher than at the 2001 general election, and for electors with previous experience of voting by post this figure was even higher. In the North East, where there have been several trials of postal voting, take-up of postal voting increased by 13.6 percentage points on 2001.

'Sam Younger, Chairman of The Electoral Commission, said: "Our research highlights the possibility that after two historically low turnout general elections some people are now out of the habit of voting, with a generation apparently carrying forward their non-voting as they get older. If the first few elections adults experience are crucial in shaping their political outlook including the value of voting, then all of us with an interest in the health of our democracy need to redouble our efforts to reverse this trend before the next general election, or we risk losing that generation for good."

'Mr Younger added: "Striking the right balance between the security of the voting system and the ease with which people can vote is very important. While postal voting seems to have helped edge up turnout, for the first time our research found more people rating it as unsafe than safe. We believe that a system of individual registration would strike the right balance and should be introduced as soon as possible so that the register used at the next general election is secure, accurate and commands public confidence".'

Source F: 'Now the silliness is over, Tories must be assertive', Daily Telegraph, 28 September 2005
'The Conservative Party has been dancing on the brink, but it has recoiled – just. The leg represented by the MPs swung merrily over the edge, but the more solidly planted voluntary party held firm. Michael Howard's changes to the leadership election rules were accepted by a majority of volunteers, but not by quite enough to make the two thirds he needed.

'The rebels are to be congratulated on their courage in standing up to Mr Howard. If his plans had passed, it would have been the first time in modern Western political history that a party, having granted democracy, succeeded in clawing it back. It speaks of the profound confusion that has long prevailed in the Conservative Party that its leaders, espousing the principles of freedom, accountability and localism, should simultaneously seek to restrict power in their own party to a handful of politicians in Westminster.

'It is certainly true, as Mr Howard and his party chairman, Francis Maude, have argued, that the membership of the Tory party is somewhat unrepresentative of the country as a whole. Yet in the name of broadening its appeal, they were proposing to restrict the franchise to fewer than 200 individuals, almost all of them male, white and from the professional classes. The reform would have left Scotland represented by one voter and Wales by three, and entirely disfranchised most of the major cities outside London.

'The response to the "unrepresentativeness" of the local party is not to take power away from the members, but to widen their number and extend power more broadly among local voters. There is, for instance, no reason why only paid-up card-carriers should get to vote on the nomination for parliamentary candidates; as in the United States, an "open primary" system would allow any local voter not actually a member of a rival party to have his say – and thereby ensure that candidates appealed to the floating voter. If they had the courage to broaden the franchise, the Conservatives could lead the way to a more open and democratic style of politics.'

To what extent and why does enthusiasm for further democratic reform seem to have died away since 2001?

This has, indeed, become a common practice in parts of the United States where, in more than half the states, a petition of citizens can trigger off an official referendum through the 'initiative' system; and, in California alone, nearly 200 propositions have been settled by public vote since the 1970s. In Britain, referendums have been used to resolve a variety of especially contentious or fundamental issues, ranging from our role in the European Union, the status of Northern Ireland and devolution to Scotland and Wales, to Sunday opening of pubs in previously 'dry' areas. By 1997, a party had been formed for the sole purpose of demanding a referendum on Britain's relationship with Europe. It is argued that such referendums can not only give unshakeable democratic authority to a decision, but are also preceded by campaigns that invigorate and inform the public, generating a democratic spirit of participation. Within little more than a year of Tony Blair's government taking office, four such referendums had been held, in which over six million people in Scotland, Wales, Northern Ireland and London voted, and a further three national referendums (on entry to the single European currency, ratification of the European Constitution and the adoption of a new electoral system for the Commons) were promised at various stages. Local referendums have been held to determine the fates of selective schools and council housing estates.

Despite this activity and enthusiasm, British politicians have been reluctant to use referendums. Clement Attlee, for all his commitment to democracy referred to in the introduction to this book, said that 'I could not consent to the introduction into our national life of a device so alien to all our traditions as the referendum, which has only too often been the instrument of Nazism and Fascism', and called referendums 'the device of demagogues and dictators'. The advantages to democracy of the referendum seem obvious: what are the drawbacks?

1. Apathy damages the authority of the result. The evidence suggests that most citizens are quickly prone to boredom with single issues and, if called upon to vote more often, simply do so in smaller numbers. Asked to spend the necessary hours reading referendum literature or watching dull, if informative, television debates, many voters might echo Oscar Wilde's conclusion that 'the trouble with socialism is that it takes up too many evenings' and Lord Hailsham's opinion that 'the man who puts politics first is not fit to be called a civilised being'. The turnouts in the referendums to establish the Welsh Assembly in 1997 (50.1 per cent) and the London Mayoralty in 1998 (34.1 per cent) hardly suggested widespread enthusiasm or gave a compelling mandate to the institutions. Outside London, the referendums for the establishment of directly elected mayors in other town and cities have hardly ever attracted turnouts of greater than 25 per cent, and the referendum on a regional assembly for the North-east achieved a figure of only 46 per cent, despite using all-postal voting. Figures from over a dozen American, European and Australian countries since World War II show that average turnouts for referendums are as much as 30 per cent below (and never above) those for elections – even in countries where voting is compulsory. In the United States, states and districts using frequent ballots commonly find that turnout is reduced to under 5 per cent. Under these circumstances, policy can be manipulated by a very unrepresentative, self-selecting group.

2. The question put to the public may be inappropriate or unclear. Many issues do not lend themselves to simple 'Yes/No' responses but even those that do are not easily resolved by use of a single referendum question because the exact meaning of a 'Yes' response may not be any more clear than the nature of the mandate granted by a vote for a party at an election. The only nationwide referendum to date in Britain asked: 'Do you think that the United Kingdom should stay in the European Community?'; and, though two-thirds of the 60 per cent turnout voted 'Yes' in 1975, the argument has raged ever since as to what the nature of our relationship should be with the institutions of the European Union, and a party was founded in 1996 with the express purpose of demanding another referendum on the same issue. Likewise, though 71 per cent of the 81 per cent turnout in the referendum on the Good Friday Agreement in Northern Ireland voted 'Yes' in May 1998, the accusation of betraying that majority is now exchanged between Unionist and Republican camps, because consent to the agreement itself does not indicate the exact order in which the parts of the agreement were intended by those voting to be fulfilled. In some referendums, the issue has even been unclear at the time of voting: it was widely acknowledged, for instance, that the French referendums on the Maastricht Treaty in September 1992 and the European Constitution in 2005 were reflections in part of the unpopularity of the incumbent President; likewise, the majority in favour of EEC membership in Britain in 1975 may be partly a reflection of the fact that the leading members of all parties had appealed to voters for a 'Yes' vote. The powers to set the question and arrange the timing of the vote are very important ones but at least they are in the hands of identifiable and accountable people; the power to interpret the answer is still more important, and everyone believes themselves possessed of it.

3. Opinions formed by the general public are likely to be more volatile and less informed than those of professional politicians or experts. Chancellor Kenneth Clarke argued against a British referendum over the Maastricht Treaty on the grounds that he himself had not read it and could not therefore reasonably expect that any of his constituents had done so. Similar arguments were pursued by government supporters seeking initially to resist a referendum on the European Constitution in 2004. This reflects Madison's arguments for representative democracy as a means of filtering out those less capable of forming stable and responsible judgements, and focusing that responsibility upon a small number of accountable and experienced politicians relying upon expert bureaucratic support. It can scarcely be disputed that most of the public would be in a weak position to decide upon the merits of competing types of nuclear reactor, for instance, or even the virtues of establishing an independent committee for determining the Bank of England's interest rate (itself a process that took economic policy even further away from democratic control). These and a thousand other daily decisions are ones that, if public interests and policy preferences are to be loyally pursued, must be limited to a very small body of persons in just the way that Mill and Schumpeter foresaw would become necessary in a technologically advanced society.

Perhaps more worrying is the prospect of such ignorance being let loose on issues concerned with privacy, the rule of law or equal treatment in areas such as race. It is not helpful to justice or social order that the majority of citizens expresses a view prejudicial towards a particular minority group, in class, ethnic or other terms. It is interesting to note that local referendums in Switzerland in March 2000 have refused citizenship to all applicants from the Balkans while granting it to all others. Whether the majority would have supported the immigration policies pursued by governments in the 1960s and 1970s, in areas such as the West Midlands or East London, is by no means certain, or on asylum in the last ten years, although the reversal of such policies might have been cruel or even racist. Those who favour referendums on such sensitive issues must ask themselves whether they are prepared to accept illiberal outcomes from them: if they promote the use of referendums on the grounds that such outcomes are inconceivable, then why hold the referendums at all?

4. Referendums undermine the democratic legitimacy of Parliament. Margaret Thatcher's objection to the referendum which was eventually held in 1975 was that it would 'bind and fetter parliamentary sovereignty'. Although technically entitled to ignore the outcome of the referendum, it was in practice clear that the Commons would be left with no room for manoeuvre on the basic issue of British membership of the EEC after the vote. Some parliamentarians saw this as an abandonment of their duty by our representatives, and an effective curtailment of their successors in contravention of the doctrine of sovereignty. The repeated use of referendums would certainly rob the Commons of some of its role as a legislative and representative chamber and, when Parliament and a referendum result (even a dated one) come into conflict (as sometimes seemed the case on Europe under the last years of John Major's government), democrats are unsure of where to look for guidance.

5. Referendums are not 'direct democracy' in the Athenian sense. The experience of voting in a referendum is qualitatively different from that which must have been enjoyed by the citizens of Athens, because there is none of what Benjamin Barber has called 'horizontal' debate – that is, discussion between citizen and citizen. With no collective meeting at which to air questions, citizens have only a 'vertical' relationship with political leaders to rely upon for an exploration of the arguments – and a markedly one-way relationship at that. We receive leaflets on the issues, see broadcasts on the television, but only rarely have the chance to challenge politicians directly: Tony Blair's uncomfortable confrontation with Sharon Storer outside a Birmingham hospital during the 2001 election campaign, and his conversation with a critical student at Leeds University in front of cameras, are rare exceptions. For writers such as Rousseau, the idea of the General Will was something that emerged from participation in the running of the state, rather than merely passing judgement on those who do, whether that judgement is passed issue by issue or only at election times.

6. The timing of referendums is determined by politicians. It is not by coincidence that the vast majority of large-scale referendums in Britain have produced 'Yes' results: they were proposed by governments under circumstances favourable to the adoption of the government's policy – most obviously when the referendum on Welsh devolution in 1997 was set a week after the Scottish one in the hope that the expected 'Yes' result in the first vote would boost the morale of the Welsh campaign in what was known to be a much more narrow contest. Issues which are unlikely to have a favourable response – such the entry into the single currency or the signing of the Maastricht Treaty – are either not raised or not put to referendums. The resources available to different campaigns may not be equal, either. In the proposed EU Constitution referendum of 2005, for example, the government would have been free to spend on the campaign from a considerably earlier date than their opponents.

The use of referendums in Britain has had many aims other than the expression of public opinion: most often it has been a means of resolving an issue on which the governing party is chronically split (such as Europe), or of entrenching a policy thought likely to be repealed by a future government unless endorsed by public vote (as with devolution in 1997). This is why such votes are unlikely to be commonplace in future; just as there are better reasons for holding referendums, however, there are also more fundamental ones for fearing their casualisation.

The state of British democracy is a cause neither for complacency nor for despondency: much has been said both to exaggerate its erst-while health and to underestimate its persistence. This has been a pre-liminary outline of the main debates about the condition of British politics, and it has bypassed some important developing questions, including the effects upon British democracy of globalisation and devolution, and the issues surrounding the running of, and access to, the mass media. These are issues considered in other titles in this series. Even this brief account, however, throws light on some import-ant topical arguments.

Many on the Left spent the latter years of the twentieth century bemoaning the loss of civic spirit, sense of solidarity and collective purpose that had once existed in Britain, accusing the Thatcher gov-ernment of 'promoting the exit of human concerns from politics'. In the words of Professor Zygmunt Bauman: 'It offers the public a massive programme of buying oneself out, singly or severally, from politics; of making politics irrelevant to the pursuit of individual or collective goals and ideas.' Bauman looked forward with scepticism to a change of government: 'Labour faces a formidable task. The nation is to be made again into a political body. Private individuals are to become citizens. Democracy is to mean again political par-ticipation, not freedom from politics'.[8] Special concern was directed at the neglect and alienation of particular groups such as the Scots governed by a Tory Party for which only a quarter of them had voted, women, or young voters of whom a 1995 study concluded that 'an entire generation has opted out of party politics'.[9]

On the free-market Right, there has been some jubilation that the enthusiasm for democratic participation is being replaced by consumerism. Noreena Hertz of the Judge Institute of Management Studies at Cambridge University scorned the falling turnout at elections while over a million people voted as to whether Kellogg's 'Choco Krispies' should revert to the name 'Coco Pops':

> Consumer politics is the real new politics we are buying, not the false new politics of devolution, coalition or proportional representation. A fundamental change is happening. As the century turns, politics as we have long known it has grown too old to rejuvenate. Politics is dead – long live the consumer.[10]

Three points should be made to dampen such excitement: firstly, most major studies of participation in Britain in the late twentieth century showed that, though political activity and loyalties are changing, they are not in overall decline – indeed, participation may be increasing in certain respects. This was the conclusion reached by the British Political Participation Study (Parry et al., 1992) which showed that a third of people believed they could exercise influence over MPs as individuals and that, as part of an organised group, two-thirds of citizens felt that they would exercise some influence. Thus, the authors concluded that 'feelings of political efficacy are fairly widely held in the population at large'.[11] The British Social Attitudes survey three years later corroborated this broadly optimistic view, demonstrating that, while only a quarter of the public participated in anything more politically active than voting, more felt they would take part in the political process if they felt it necessary, and were confident that they could influence policy if they did. Significantly, a larger number of the public expressed a willingness to sign petitions, contact politicians or the media, and join pressure groups than had done so in five parallel studies over the preceding twelve years, suggesting that political consciousness and willingness to engage in the British system of democracy were growing in the late twentieth century.[12]

What you should have learnt from reading this chapter

- Professor Kenneth Newton, who discovered so many book titles critical of liberal democracy, came to the conclusion that there is no major crisis in Western democracy, and that supposed evidence of direct challenge to established constitutions usually consists of tiny bands of extremists committed to single-issue campaigns, such as the IRA, the Baader-Meinhof gang, ETA or the Brigate Rosse. Newton told a conference in 1993 that there was no pattern of disillusionment, but rather 'a Jackson Pollock picture. The only generalisation you can make is that there are no generalisations . . . As often as not, worrying signs of pathology reverse themselves.'[13]

- Secondly, it is mistaken to believe that democracy as an ideal form can be perfectly enshrined in any set of processes or institutions: Britain cannot be governed by a single mandate from the people, but only at best by a series of competing mandates expressed through Parliament, parties, pressure groups, local government, the media and elsewhere. There is no objectively identifiable voice of 'the people' because institutions are imperfect and the people do not, in any case, speak with one unequivocal voice. To some extent, indeed, the establishment of new centres of power merely confuses the search for public sovereignty and disrupts the evolution of already successful institutions.

- In all of these matters, we must remember that democracy (even if it could be evoked in full) is not a universal cure to the ills of public policy. In all institutions, the authority of expertise, experience, individual rights and tradition can make claims to preservation; and in most institutions, it will from time to time be defended by even the most fervent self-appointed promoters of democracy. There are occasions when faith in democracy is confused with the hope that the public shares our values. 'There is', wrote Adam and Jack Lively in the notes to their documentary reader on British democracy, 'not the same tradition in British literature of celebrating "democracy" as a broad, almost aesthetic idea that there is, for example, in America'.[14] That this is true in practice is clear from what we have seen: doubtless there are historical reasons for it; it may also reflect a characteristically resigned and fatalistic British attitude to political events. There are also some equally compelling and very contemporary reasons to keep the idea of democracy firmly in its context.

Glossary of key terms

Devolution The 'loaning' of power from Parliament to other institutions covering smaller areas of the United Kingdom.

Modernisation The reform of institutions to meet changes in circumstances. This is often felt by critics to be the government's euphemism for centralisation.

Likely examination questions

Have the Blair governments produced the constitutional 'revolution' that was promised in 1997?

How could parties be reformed so as to perform their functions better?

Should we accept that the Prime Minister has now become a presidential figure?

How could the wider use of referendums or citizens' juries improve British government?

Helpful websites

This website, run by the University College London Constitution Unit, provides a running commentary on constitutional reforms

www.ucl.ac.uk/constitution-unit/index.php

Suggestions for further reading

Graham Allen, *The Last Prime Minister. Being Honest about the UK Presidency* (Imprint Academic, 2001) (also available at www.grahamallen.labour.co.uk).

T. Benn and A. Hood, *Common Sense: a New Constitution for Britain* (Hutchinson, 1993).

Neil Smith, 'New Labour and Constitutional Reform', *Talking Politics*, September 2001.

Keith Sutherland, *The Party's Over: Blueprint for a Very English Revolution* (Imprint Academic, 2004).

Alan Trench (ed.), *Has Devolution Made a Difference? The State of the Nations 2004* (Imprint Academic, 2004).

Stuart Weir and David Beetham, *Political Power and Democratic Control in Britain: The Democratic Audit of the United Kingdom* (Routledge, 1999).

CHAPTER 7

Conclusion: The Puzzle of Participation

Contents

Overview

The conclusion examines one of the most regularly discussed questions of British democratic life in recent years: why has the number of people voting declined and what, if anything, ought to be done to reverse this trend? Five competing explanations for this phenomenon are set out, their strengths and weaknesses evaluated and their implications for parties, government, media and public considered. This debate is set in the context of the theoretical ideas examined in Part I of this book.

Key issues

- What is the role of voting in various theoretical conceptions of democracy?
- What has been the pattern of turnout in recent British elections?
- What explanations have been offered for this pattern?
- What responses do the different explanations suggest would be appropriate, and from whom?
- What are the strengths and weaknesses of these explanations?

The first half of this book is concerned with the reasons that might in principle, make democracy and participation valuable, or the circumstances under which they might be valuable. The Athenian general and statesman, Pericles (c. 495–429 BC), thought it was each citizen's duty to vote; Rousseau believed that it would release our sense of communal identity and common interest; Madison hoped it would restrain overpowerful government; Mill that it would lead to a more educated and responsible public mind. All of these, and even pessimistic twentieth-century Competitive Élitists, whose chief interest was order and efficiency, argue that, in some way, public participation is necessary to give legitimacy to government. They take irreconcilably different views about the level and type of participation required to lend authority to government and about the power it legitimises, but they all regard the vote, in some form or other, as a minimum act or entitlement for a system to qualify as democracy.

It is the decline of this form of participation that has been the subject of widespread concern and enquiry in Britain in recent years. After the 2001 general election, newspapers as diverse as the *Guardian* and the *Sunday Express* warned their readers to 'Be alarmed by apathy' and 'Beware of extremists who thrive on apathy' in editorials on consecutive days. William Hague's immediate reaction to the result was that 'it must be a very sobering lesson for all parties that millions of people have been reluctant, or have refused to participate in this election at all'. The Electoral Commission's report of the results claimed that 'identifying and addressing the causes of low turnout is a key challenge facing the UK's political system and leaders'.[1] Despite a constitution giving pride of place to the elected chamber of its sovereign Parliament, and a recent programme of reform opening up a plethora of new ways to vote and new institutions for which to vote, the British public seems to have gone off the idea. Having lost faith in the established parties, they now appear to have lost interest in the electoral process: those voters who are not turning to the minor parties are often not turning out at all. Whereas between 1945 and 1970 the average turnout at general elections was 77.5 per cent, during 1974–92 it was 75.4 per cent, and in 1997 it reached a post-war low of 71.4 per cent, so that Blair's 'landslide' was actually won on half a million fewer votes than Major's narrow victory of 1992. In 2001 this trend was accelerated so that only 59.4 per cent of those entitled to vote did so and, for the first time, more people – almost twice as many, in fact – failed to vote than voted for the winning party. Despite widespread use of postal voting (with accompanying controversies about the security of the votes cast), this figure rose to only 61.3 per cent in 2005 – the second lowest figure since 1918, the lowest being 2001.

Nor were general elections the only signal of this trend: turnout declined in parliamentary by-elections and, in June 1999, there was for the first time the dubious spectacle of an MP returned for Leeds Central after a poll in which less than a fifth of the electorate had participated. The turnout at the Scottish parliamentary elections fell from 59 per cent in 1999 to 49 per cent in 2003; in Welsh Assembly elections from 46 per cent to 38 per cent in the same years. Most notoriously of all, the European elections of 1999 showed an all-time low for a national election of 24 per cent of the electorate bothering to vote. Although this figure was restored to a more respectable 38 per cent for the 2004 European elections, this involved the use of all-postal voting in four English regions, with the commensurate questionability of the seriousness and security of the votes cast. Few serious analyses of this process have regarded it in an entirely sanguine way, and most have acknowledged that a range of factors is likely to be involved. These reflect the range of pessimistic and optimistic analyses reviewed in Part I of this book, and include the following:

The 'politics of contentment'

The most optimistic explanation for the low turnout at recent elections is that it reflects public satisfaction with the general running of the country and the performance of the economy. Low turnout is essentially the responsibility of the voters. Citizens, having no serious grievances to air, and feeling no great threat of change (either because the party of government would not change or because, if it did, the running of the country would not change) had no motivation to vote unless they were strong partisans. This argument was put as long ago as the 1960s by Peter Pulzer who pointed out, in *Political Representation and Elections in Britain*, that high turnouts often signify dysfunction and instability in political systems as, for example, in later Weimar Germany. The same might be said, for example, of the high turnouts commonly witnessed in Northern Ireland elections. Conversely, Pulzer argued, 'apparently apathetic behaviour . . . may reflect widespread acceptance of the way in which disputes are resolved'.[2] After the 2001 election, Tony Travers, Director of the London School of Economics Greater London Group, acknowledged the possibility that voters may have been thinking 'good wages, good economy, steady growth, so why change anything?'[3] but it was politicians, unsurprisingly mainly members of the government, who have referred most explicitly to the 'politics of contentment'. This was the explanation offered by Peter Hain and John Prescott for low turnout by Labour supporters at the first Welsh Assembly elections in 1999; and after the 2001 result, Jack Straw told the BBC that 'The politics of contentment may be a factor in low turnout: we will find after the election there are loads more people who wanted a Labour victory than actually turned out to vote. So the state of the moral authority will paradoxically be greater than that of the vote.' This argument shares much ground with the Schumpeterian outlook, giving only a peripheral, perhaps even implicit, role to voters and suggesting that the political and social systems can run healthily without their participation.

Reassuring as this may be to ministers, there are good reasons to doubt whether it was the explanation for low turnout on this occasion. First of all, other evidence, notably that of opinion polls on policy issues and trust in government, did not suggest unusually widespread contentment; in fact, they – and the events of the campaigns, such as constant attacks upon ministers over the state of the education and health services, and the election and re-election of Independent MP, Richard Taylor, suggested quite the reverse. The second Blair term of office was overshadowed by visible mass opposition to the war in Iraq, and an associated collapse of public trust in the administration. It is surely implausible to claim that the public is more content with the Labour government now than when it was first returned in 1997; but that is what the 'contentment' thesis suggests. Indeed, if low turnout signifies satisfaction with the way public affairs are being managed, then it is by and large the most deprived constituencies which have the most contented populations: the wooden spoon for turnout went in 2001 and in 2005 to Liverpool Riverside (34.1 per cent and 41.4 per cent), and thirty of the bottom thirty-one seats by turnout were

Labour-held in 2001; all of the bottom ten in 2005. In 2005, non-voters accounted for 30 per cent of the professional and managerial classes, but 46 per cent of manual labourers in classes D and E; the turnout in the average Labour seat was 7 per cent below that for the average Conservative seat. The 'contentment' thesis suggests that we are happiest with the management of European Union affairs; next happiest with local government, followed by the Scottish Parliament and Welsh Assemblies; and that only the conduct of the House of Commons worries enough of us to raise turnout to above 50 per cent. Clearly, this cannot be the whole story, and it is suspiciously convenient for those in power even as a main factor. Andrew Marr dismissed the syndrome sarcastically as 'Prozac politics' – short-term inertia which ministers mistake for a satisfaction rating. 'If fierce political argument is the sign of an unhappy country', Marr mused in 1999, 'this must be the happiest Britain in living memory. It must be one of the happiest countries in the world.'[4]

The 'foregone conclusion' argument

This is in some ways a more specific version of the 'contentment' case. It was argued after 2001 and 2005 (and feared before those elections) by some government supporters that those elections would be so predictably comprehensive victories that many potential voters – Labour and Conservative, in fact – would doubt whether their vote would have any impact on the result. Thus, the responsibility for low turnout lay chiefly with the Opposition for not trying hard enough. This was the basis of a warning given by Tony Blair to a special cabinet meeting in January 2001, and the motivation for the 'Big Choice' theme struck by Labour in 2005. After the election, some analysts used the evidence of higher turnout in more marginal seats to give support to this theory after the results came in: Andrew Geddes and Jonathan Tonge concluded that,

> . . . the variation in turnout according to marginality of constituency offers some indication of people making rational choices about whether to vote. Labour's superior performances where it mattered indicate how this was a latent Labour landslide in addition to being an actual one. It suggests Labour had a 'reserve' army of support to call upon had the party's election victory appeared under threat.[5]

As if to demonstrate this, the highest mainland British turnout in 2005 was for Dorset West, the highly marginal and hotly contested seat of Shadow Chancellor, Oliver Letwin. Jack Straw was again keen to seize upon this comforting explanation after the 2001 election, accusing the press of 'discounting the result of this election for weeks and weeks and weeks', and saying that the message he had heard on the doorsteps from an 'awful lot of people' was: 'Yes, I am with you, of course I would turn out if it really mattered, but I think it is already won.'

Once again, however, though plausible, this explanation looks less convincing when set against the detail of general election results and in the context of other elections over time. Correlation between levels of marginality and turnout is a common feature of elections and, if more pronounced recently, may well reflect the more ruthless strategy of targeting employed by parties: the greater the number of canvassers, newspaper advertisements and front-bench visits a constituency receives, the greater is likely to be its turnout, marginal or not. But it is, of course, marginal seats that enjoy these experiences most fully at election times. Even the parties' targeting, however, did not raise marginal turnout to average levels: in the sixty-eight seats with majorities of less than 5 per cent in 2001, an average of 64.4 per cent of the public voted, well below the national average for all seats of 71.4 per cent in the (post-war record low) 1997 election. The highest mainland constituency figure – for Winchester – was only just above the 1997 average, at 72.3 per cent. Geoffrey Evans argued in 2003 that the solution to poor turnout was 'the re-emergence of an effective opposition' and that 'if the Conservatives gradually recover support, as we might expect, or the Liberal Democrats increase their vote, then subsequent general elections could be regarded as closer contests, and turnout can be expected to increase.'[6]

Yet, in these terms, the 2005 contest brings the 'foregone conclusion' case further into question. The 'Big Choice' produced the closest-run outcome in terms of the popular vote of the two main parties (a mere 3 per cent) since February 1974, and the closest three-way split in the vote since the 1920s; the Prime Minister's constant reminders to Labour supporters that Michael Howard could win were confirmed by polls in which the Conservatives consistently snapped at Labour's heels, and proved to be close to the mark in the real outcome, but this did not persuade many more of them to vote than had done so in 2001. Conversely, the largest margins of victory for a winning party in recent general elections – 15 per cent in 1983 and 11 per cent in 1987 – could not conceivably have been in doubt at any point in the campaign, and yet the turnout at those contests was 72.7 per cent and 75.3 per cent. Predictability might be enough to put people off voting but we still need to explain why it used not to. Moreover, the comparable decline of turnout in other elections undermines the whole idea of the foregone conclusion: why, for example, did turnout fall when Labour lost national elections to the Conservatives in 1999 for the European Parliament, in local elections at which Labour was under serious threat, or in parliamentary by-election contests, such as Brent East and Leicester South, where the Liberal Democrats made gains? The 'foregone conclusion' factor has a superficial appeal as an explanation for the last two general elections: it does not explain why voters of all parties stay at home when their party is under threat, though they used to vote when it was assured of victory.

The 'lack of choice' argument

Sections of Chapter 5 of this book referred to the problem of party crossover in ideological terms, and it is possible that lower turnout at recent elections can be explained in terms of Downsian electoral theory, given that all parties – especially the two main ones – are crowded into a relatively small part of the political spectrum. The responsibility for low turnout in this case lies with all parties. All including, lately, the Liberal Democrats – accept the base rate of income tax established by the Thatcher and Major governments; all (including, reluctantly, the Conservatives) acknowledge the minimum wage and the referendum results on devolution; all accept that the United Kingdom is a member state of the European Union but are disinclined to go any further towards economic or political integration without referendum approval. It can be argued that this convergence has produced an apolitical confrontation at elections which gives voters little choice and therefore little reason to make a choice. Former Labour government adviser, David Clark, pointed in 2004 to 'strong evidence . . . in the substantial rise in the number of voters who see little difference between the parties'.[7] During the 1997 election campaign, an NOP poll for the *Sunday Times* found that 60 per cent of voters thought that there was 'not much difference' between the main parties or that they were 'much the same', and that 42 per cent thought that the election would make only a little difference, or none at all. British Election Study figures show that, in 1983, only 7 per cent of voters saw 'not much' difference between the parties, whereas the figure was 24 per cent in 1997 and 44 per cent in 2001. Turnout among weak party identifiers in this group had been especially poor. A YouGov poll for the *Daily Telegraph* two months before to the 2005 general election found that, though 43 per cent of respondents thought the two main parties were 'very different', 41 per cent – a figure curiously correspondent to the non-voting rates at the previous and following general elections – thought that Labour and the Conservatives were 'much of a muchness'.

There are some major methodological problems in deciding how plausible this theory is: for example, is a perceived similarity between parties the same as an actual one? Is a policy similarity the same as a similarity of identity in terms of image or identity? Setting all of that aside however, this is another explanation that suffers when placed in recent historical context: it is true that the contests between the radical alternatives of New Right, militarist Thatcherism and unilaterialist, Clause IV Labour inspired higher turnouts in the 1980s; but then so did the choice between post-Policy Review Kinnock and moderate Major in 1992 – and all the general elections of the

---

Box 7.1 Turnout at recent elections in percentage of electorate

	1992–7	1997–2001	2001–05
General elections	71	59	61*
European elections	36	24	38**
Parliamentary by-elections	51	39	40

* Proportion of votes cast by post rose from 5 per cent to 15 per cent
** All-postal voting in use in four English regions

How do we account for the decline in participation at British elections?

'Butskellite' era of the 1950s and 1960s, when the two main parties disagreed about little more then the exact scale of progressive taxation and the expansion of the welfare state. All sorts of ideological struggles, Titanic and anodyne, have attracted bigger voter participation than those of the twenty-first century. Consensus may be a reason for non-voting, and voters may believe it to be: but we are left wondering why it was not a good enough reason in the past.

The 'alienation' argument

The responsibility for non-voting in this theory is not merely with the party leaders and their policies at any particular election, but with political processes on all occasions. Non-voting is not merely a political shrug of the public shoulders when faced with a policy question, it is a two-fingered gesture in the face of the political establishment – a deliberate gesture intended to indicate positive withdrawal from the electoral charade. There is a wealth of evidence that increasing numbers of citizens simply do not trust politicians, do not believe in elections generally, or at least do not believe that they are significant. In the same 1997 *Sunday Times* poll which showed most people saw little difference between the parties, politicians topped the list of professionals least admired by the public, ahead of journalists, estate agents, social workers and lawyers. Thus, even if they had made diametrically opposed promises, they would not have been believed. Michael Brown wrote in the *Independent* on 6 June 2002 that 'there is a growing feeling of alienation which is coupled with the view that the politicians are not listening to the people. This is bringing all forms of democracy into a considerable measure of disrepute.' The 2001 British Social Attitudes Survey is one source of evidence for this theory of 'crisis': whereas in 1987 only 48 per cent of respondents agreed that 'people like me have no say in what government does', this figure had risen to 57 per cent by 1997 and 66 per cent in 2001. Whereas 55 per cent had thought politicians were 'only interested in people's votes, not their opinions' in 1987, by 2001 this had risen to 76 per cent. According to *Social Trends 33*, the proportion of respondents who 'just about always' or 'most of the time' trusted British governments fell from 39 per cent in 1974 to 16 per cent in 2000. Although there had been a quite generous honeymoon period after

1997, when trust in government, and particularly the Prime Minister, had been unusually high, accusations surrounding British entry into the Iraq war, and resentment at limited progress in improving welfare services, had soured the relationship again by 2005, especially among young voters, whose willingness to vote has always lagged behind that of their seniors. This was not an analysis to be found only in radical or anti-establishment circles. Leader of the Commons, Geoff Hoon, offered his reflections on the 2005 election at a speech to the Institute for Public Policy Research:

> What I witnessed during the campaign among some sections of society was not apathy. It was not sloth – as I heard suggested recently. It was not always the politics of contentment, much as it might suit me to think so. No, it was – what seems today to be an old-fashioned word – alienation. The feeling among many people that their vote will not change anything. The perception that decisions taken in Parliament make no difference to their lives. This is not apathy. I found when I talked to non-voters that they raised a whole set of issues and grievances. But they did not see how voting would affect them one way or another.[8]

Is there a crisis of British democracy characterised by rejection of parliamentary elections, and the growth of extra-parliamentary and even anti-parliamentary pressure-group activity ranging from the poll tax riots to the 'stop the war' protests or refusal to pay petrol or council taxes? This is the sort of outcome of representative democracy envisaged ultimately by socialist and Marxist writers from Rousseau onwards. If so, this would be a distressing but not irremediable situation: after all, parties and government institutions (and perhaps the media and pressure groups) could seek ways to reconnect with the public, some of which are explored in Chapter 6. A certain leap of faith would be required by governors and by governed, but one which has been made successfully in what were potentially far more revolutionary circumstances in Britain's history (such as the Reform Acts of 1832 and 1867, the Edwardian Liberal reforms, or perhaps the General Strike of 1926). Geoffrey Evans argues that this explanation is misconceived, because the period of sharpest decline in voting has been concurrent with relatively stable levels of commitment to the idea of voting as a civic duty. Moreover, the scale and durability of 'anti-system' campaigns – or, far that matter, parties such as the BNP – have been far too limited to constitute evidence of a widespread rejection of parliamentary methods. Interestingly, surveys conducted by MORI after the 2001 elections showed that most non-voters usually gave practical reasons for not having turned out, over half saying that voting was 'inconvenient' (21 per cent), that they were 'away' (16 per cent), 'too busy' (6 per cent) or 'had no polling card' (11 per cent). Whether honest or not (it is, for example, not necessary to present a polling card when voting, and more polling stations had been opened than before, and postal voting made easier for the sake of convenience) these responses reflect a certain embarrassment at not voting more than a direct rejection of the alternative choices or the process itself. Responses such as 'Didn't like parties' (5 per cent), 'Didn't like candidates' (4 per cent), 'Vote wouldn't have made a difference' (2 per cent) and 'Don't think voting is important' (1 per cent) were unpopular. Hypocrisy, it is said, is the compliment vice pays to virtue: even if it is being disingenuous, the British public knows what virtue is.

The 'social capital' argument

This explanation does not place blame for declining turnout so much as see it as an outcome of social and economic change. It therefore leaves the advocates of British parliamentary democracy with the biggest dilemma of all. It has long been recognised by political scientists that, in raw instrumental terms, especially in the first-past-the-post electoral system, voting is often an irrational practice. Most votes have no real prospect of affecting the result, and many who vote have only a peripheral interest in the outcome anyway. In a study of non-voting between 1966 and 1974, this was acknowledged by Crewe, Fox and Alt, who went on to explain why people usually do still vote:

> Voting is an overwhelmingly 'easy' form of political participation. It barely requires any individual effort, initiative, skill or sacrifice. It does not engage the participant in conflict-laden or co-operative relations with others. And a high value is attached to it in the country and by almost all social groups.[9]

The 'social capital' argument explains increased turnout by pointing to the fact that, in relative terms, voting is no longer regarded as being as 'easy' as it once was; and that the social pressure to vote is no longer as intense as it was when Crewe et al. were writing. Technologically, 'easy' has come to mean phone texting, clicking on a mouse or a digital-television remote control; and social pressures from family, work and friends have dispersed. The family is no longer as uniform and stable a structure as it once was; work is more flexible from day to day and changeable from year to year; and the host of contexts through which friendship was supported, particularly among the politically literate – whether that was working men's clubs, churches or the local school – have been undermined by home entertainment, individual materialism and geographical mobility. The communal features of our lifestyles and our identity have gone, and with them the incentive to undertake even that minimal participation of voting. Voting was in large part a social activity, and now the society which made it seem natural, and the expectations which perpetuated it, have to some extent disappeared. This analysis was most famously set out in Robert Putnam's 2001 book, *Bowling Alone*, which sought to show how the sort of civic culture which had underpinned American democracy, and was recognised in Dahl's *Who Governs?* and Almond and Verba's *The Civic Culture* (1963), was in measurable decline, and that the more the activities associated with it (such as the apparently minor example of team bowling) went into decline, the more turnout fell.

> Television, two-career families, suburban sprawl, generational changes in values – these and other changes in American society have meant that fewer and fewer of us find that the League of Women Voters, or the United Way, or the Shriners, or the monthly bridge club, or even a Sunday picnic with friends fits the way we have come to live. Our growing social-capital deficit threatens educational performance, safe neighbourhoods, equitable tax collection, democratic responsiveness, everyday honesty, and even our health and happiness.[10]

Paul Whitely, among others, has come to some similar conclusions about 'good citizenship' as a basis for turnout in Britain, and has used it to explain why Scandanavia has been relatively protected from the turnout decline that has taken place across Europe. An example of the common values arising out of common experience of British voters which is dying off is the belief in the civic duty to vote, which is markedly stronger in pensioners than among first-time voters.

These arguments resonate with the logic of Communitarianism and Rousseau's *Social Contract* seen in Chapter 3. The attempt to recreate community is one possible reaction to this analysis – although, given the powerful social and economic forces which have weakened our commitment to vote in this way, it is not surprising that Communitarianism meets some of the criticisms also reviewed there. Failing the reconstruction of social expectations, the other possible response is to revive the 'easiness' of voting using new methods: voting electronically, voting by post, voting on different days – even being compelled legally to vote, on pain of a fine. This system is used in Australia, Belgium and elsewhere, and, like the other reforms listed with it here, might improve turnout by something between 5 and 10 per cent on the basis of experience among British pilots and practice abroad. These ideas, too – particularly e-voting – met with some criticism in Chapter 2, and there is a danger that compulsory voting would go even further than postal and electronic voting in altering the meaning of the vote. To vote would no longer be to offer willingly an opinion on matters that motivated the elector; it would be to choose, perhaps fatalistically, perhaps grudgingly – even resentfully – between parties who no longer had to work to lure us out to the polling station. The results could be greater support for anti-system parties from angry former non-voters; or greater support for mainstream parties from those dragooned against their inertia by the material incentive of a fine.

Either way, few would argue that the votes thus cast would be more serious or substantial, and the mandate they offered more meaningful, than those currently given against the limited obstacles described by Crewe et al. The question of what the mandate means, set out in Chapter 5, would be made even more speculative and diverse in character. Putnam's thesis was tested by Fiona Devine in an in-depth study of over 700 voluntary activists in 2003; it found that,

> Putnam's account of social capital does not work as it is supposed to do. It is the case that associational activities are more likely to generate norms of reciprocity and trust between people with which they interact on a face-to-face basis. That said, group life is not always a positive experience and can be a source of exclusion, conflict and distrust, too. Most importantly, experiences of group life do not predispose people to be more trusting towards politicians, the political parties and government.[11]

Much of this echoes criticisms of Communitarianism voiced in Chapter 3.

Summary

So where does all this leave British democracy? On the pessimistic side, the British Westminster model was never intended to give voters more than an arm's length relationship with power and, in recent years, political attitudes and social conditions and expectations have made it an increasingly ineffective structure for achieving even that. Attempts at reform have been mishandled by politicians with centralist instincts, and resulted in lower turnouts and trust ratings than ever. On the other hand, the British Constitution continues to show its capacity for adaptation, with a bigger programme of political reform in the last decade than has been seen for nearly a century; and, outside the 'official' institutions and relationships of the Westminster model – perhaps even despite them – there is a vibrant culture of academic enquiry, public debate and practical experiment in new ideas about democracy. The Eighteenth British Social Attitudes Survey of 2001 showed that, as in two of the previous three surveys since 1989, more than half of the public had taken part in a political activity, such as writing to an MP, contacting the media or going on a demonstration. All of this confirms that, whatever the strengths and weaknesses of our key institutions, it is they – especially the parties at election time – who will restore or let fall Britain's faith in democracy. If the parties really were over, no one would devote so much energy to berating them as their critics do.

It may be trite to observe that the answer to the question 'Is Britain a Democracy?' depends firstly upon what we mean by democracy, and Part I made clear that this is a very open question. Part II demonstrated that, even within the common ground of the British cultural and political tradition, we have come to expect more, and are less prepared to be deferential about how we get it. We shop around among parties, if we vote at all, we use diverse methods to get our ideas across to one another and to government; and we have elevated material and social expectations compared with those of our parents and grandparents. Looking down the wrong end of the political telescope, from expectation to reality, British democracy looks small.

Moreover, Part I also emphasised the semi-detached relationship democracy has with most British political traditions: understandably, each wants to befriend democracy, but none will be its servant. The British political system reflects this: it provides checks and balances against the unrealistic expectations or rash urges of public opinion, feared in one way or another by conservatives, liberals and socialists. It is a characteristic example of discretion – some might say hypocrisy – that, for most people in the British political system, the fact that it is not a perfect democracy may not be a weakness, but few would say so. Whether Britain is not a democracy may not be the real issue – it may be whether Britain is not quite a democracy in the right way.

Helpful websites

This site gives detailed results of the 2005 general election:

www.parliament.uk/commons/lib/research/rp2005/rp05-033.pdf

Suggestions for further reading

Electoral Commission, *Election 2001: The Official Results* (Politico's, 2001).

References

Introduction

1. A. V. Dicey, *An Introduction to the Study of the Law of the Constitution* (Macmillan, 1959) (first published 1885).
2. C. Attlee in R. Acland (ed.), *Why I am a Democrat* (Lawrence and Wishart, 1939).
3. F. Fukuyama, *The End of History and the Last Man* (Free Press, 1992).
4. B. Crick, *Democracy*, The Schools Council General Studies Project Unit (Longman, 1974).

Chapter 1

1. H. F. Pitkin, *The Concept of Representation* (University of California Press, 1967).
2. C. B. MacPherson, *The Life and Times of Liberal Democracy* (Oxford University Press, 1977).
3. R. Hattersley, *Choose Freedom* (Michael Joseph, 1987).
4. G. Brown, *The Guardian*, 2 August 1997.
5. R. Hattersley, *The Observer*, 24 June 2001.
6. J. Harris, *So Now Who Do We Vote For?* (Faber and Faber, 2005).
7. F. Hayek, *The Road to Serfdom* (Routledge, 2001).
8. R. Nozick, *Anarchy, State and Utopia* (Blackwell, 1974).
9. M. Friedman, *Capitalism and Freedom* (University of Chicago, 2002).
10. M. and R. Friedman, *Free to Choose* (Harvest, 1990).
11. N. Tebbit, *The Values of Freedom* (Conservative Political Centre, 1985).
12. D. Willetts, *Modern Conservatism* (Penguin, 1992).

Chapter 2

1. B. Walden (presenter), 'Democracy', London Weekend Television, 1993.
2. R. Scruton, *The Case Against Democracy* (Open University audio, 1987).
3. G. C. Field, 'Democracy, Ancient and Modern', *The Cambridge Journal*, vol. III, no. 2, 1949.

4. P. Cartledge, 'Greek Lessons', *New Statesman*, 'Bite the Ballot' supplement, 1994.

5. B. Farrington, in R. Acland (ed.), op. cit.

6. A. Arblaster, *Democracy* (Open University, 1988).

7. Demos, 'Lean Democracy', *Demos Quarterly*, no. 3, 1994.

8. P. Johnson, *Wake up Britain!* (Weidenfeld and Nicolson, 1994).

9. G. Hoon, 'The End of the Affair', *IPPR*, 4 July 2005.

10. C. Barnes and K. Isaac-Henry, 'Local Government on the Line', UCE Dept of Public Policy, 1999.

11. Parliamentary Office of Science and Technology, *Electronic Government*, 1998.

12. M. Meacher, 'Political Machinations', *The Guardian*, 2 February 2005.

13. B. Barber, 'Citizens', *Greek Fire*, Channel Four, 1989.

14. J. Gray, *Digital Democracy*, BBC2, 4 July 1995.

15. I. McLean, 'Mechanisms for Democracy' in D. Held and C. Pollitt (eds) *New Forms of Democracy* (Sage, 1986).

16. A. Dilnot, *Analysis*, BBC Radio Four, 26 July 1999.

Chapter 3

1. D. Thomson, 'Rousseau and the General Will' in *Political Ideas* (Pelican, 1966).

2. J. L. Talmon, *The Origins of Totalitarian Democracy* (Secker and Warburg, 1952).

3. A. Etzioni, *The Spirit of Community* (Fontana, 1995).

4. A. Etzioni, *The Monochrome Society* (Princeton University Press, 2001).

5. A. Etzioni, *The Common Good* (Polity Press, 2004).

6. A. Blair, 'Faith in the City – 10 Years On', 26 January 1996.

7. A. Blair, 'The Third Way: Politics for the New Century', Fabian Society, 1998.

8. A. Giddens, *The Third Way* (Polity Press, 1998).

9. P. Richards, *Is the Party Over?* (Fabian Society, 2000).

10. D. Blunkett, 'Civil Renewal: a New Agenda', Edith Kahn Memorial Lecture, 11 June 2003.

11. Quoted in P. Lashmar, 'It's all for your own good', *The Guardian*, 25 September 2004.

12. A. Cochrane, 'Community Politics and Democracy' in D. Held and C. Pollitt, op. cit.

13. A. Etzioni, *The Times*, 20 February 1995 and in 'The Battle for Ideas', BBC TV, 1995.
14. S. E. Finer, *Comparative Government* (Pelican, 1970).
15. R. Dahl, *Who Governs?: Democracy and Power in an American City* (Yale University Press, 1961).
16. D. Held, *Models of Democracy* (Polity Press, 1996).
17. G. Duncan, *Marx and Mill* (Cambridge University Press, 1973).
18. A. Lively, *Parliament: the Great British Democracy Swindle* (Chatto and Windus, 1990).

Chapter 4

1. D. Kavanagh, Westminster Central Hall, 5 May 1992.
2. R. M. Punnett, *British Government and Politics* (Heinemann, 1968).
3. P. Norton in 'The State We're In', BBC TV, 5 June 1995.
4. B. Jones, 'British Democracy Today', *Talking Politics*, vol. 6, no. 3, summer 1994.
5. S. Jenkins, *Accountable to None* (Penguin, 1996).
6. S. Weir, 'Crisis of Confidence', *New Statesman*, Bite the Ballot supplement, 1994.
7. J. Fisher et al., *General Election 2005: A Voter's Eye View*, General Election Monitoring Project, 2005.
8. Q. Hogg, *The Purpose of Parliament* (Blandford Press, 1945).
9. J. Major, Centre for Policy Studies, 26 June 1996.
10. P. Hennessy, 'Whitehall and the Reforms', Politics Association video PA17, 1994.
11. Lord Denning, The Richard Dimbleby Lecture, 1980.
12. P. Taylor, *The Judiciary in the Nineties* (BBC Education, 1992).
13. P. Taylor, Newspaper Press Fund lunch, 1996.
14. R. M. Punnett, op. cit.
15. P. Webb, *The Modern Party System* (Sage, 2000).
16. C. Secrett, 'Why Society Needs Pressure Groups', in W. Waldegrave et al., *Pressure Group Politics in Modern Britain* (Social Market Foundation, 1996).
17. R. Baggot, *Pressure Groups: A Question of Interest* (PAVIC, 1993).
18. P. Norris, *A Virtuous Circle: Political Communications in Postindustrial Societies* (Cambridge University Press, 2000).

Chapter 5

1. The 1998 Jenkins Commission report can be seen at www.archive.official-documents.co.uk/document/cm40/4090/contents.htm
2. S. E. Finer, *Adversary Politics and Electoral Reform* (Anthony Wigram, 1975).
3. V. Bogdanor, *Politics and the People* (Victor Gollancz, 1997).
4. A. Geddes and J. Tonge, *Labour's Landslide* (Manchester University Press, 1997).
5. J. Harris, op. cit.
6. B. Sedgemore, *An Insider's Guide to Parliament* (Icon, 1995).
7. Lord Hailsham, *A Sparrow's Flight* (Collins, 1990).
8. M. Austin and Z. Brennan, 'Obey, obey . . .', *Sunday Times*, 29 March 1998.
9. B. Lenman, *The Eclipse of Parliament* (Edward Arnold, 1992).
10. P. Cowley, An Absence of War? New Labour in Parliament, in J. Fisher et al. (eds), *British Elections and Parties Review*, vol. 9 (Frank Cass, 1999).
11. J. Nott in '3000 Days', BBC TV, 1988.
12. R. Hattersley in 'Blair's Year', Channel Four TV, 19 April 1998.
13. M. Foley, *The British Presidency* (Manchester University Press, 2000).
14. C. Campbell and G. Wilson, *The End of Whitehall* (Blackwell, 1995).
15. J. A. G. Griffith, *The Politics of the Judiciary* (HarperCollins, 1997).
16. Quoted in *The Times*, 16 May 1995.
17. On these issues, see J. Rozenberg, *Trial of Strength* (Richard Cohen, 1997).
18. T. Blair, quoted in *The Times*, 27 July 2005.
19. K. Sutherland, *The Party's Over* (Imprint Academic, 2004).
20. P. Whiteley et al., *True Blues* (Oxford University Press, 1994).
21. P. Norris and J. Lovenduski, 'Why Parties Fail to Learn', *Party Politics*, vol. 10, no. 1 (Sage, 2004).
22. P. Richards, op. cit.
23. M. J. Smith, *Pressure Politics* (Baseline Books, 1995).
24. W. Grant, *Pressure Groups and British Politics* (Macmillan, 2000).
25. B. Franklin, *Newszak and News Media* (Arnold, 1997).

Chapter 6

1. Royal Commission on the House of Lords, A House for the Future, HMSO Cm 4534, 2000.

2. T. Benn, *Arguments for Democracy* (Penguin, 1982).
3. G. Allen, *The Last Prime Minister* (Imprint Academic, 2001).
4. D. Kavanagh, 'Bona Fide or Bonaparte?', *Times Higher Education Supplement*, 26 November 1999.
5. B. Walden, 'Kinnock's fate rests with his own MPs', *Sunday Times*, 1988.
6. A. Ware, 'Political Parties' in D. Held and C. Politt, op. cit.
7. B. Beedham, 'A Better Way to Vote', *The Economist*, 11 September 1993.
8. Z. Bauman, 'Britain's Exit from Politics', *New Statesman*, 29 July 1988.
9. H. Wilkinson and G. Mulgan, *Freedom's Children* (Demos, 1995).
10. N. Hertz, 'Better to Shop than to Vote', *New Statesman*, 21 June 1999.
11. G. Parry, G. Moyser and N. Day, *Political Participation and Democracy in Britain* (Cambridge University Press, 1992).
12. J. Curtice and R. Jowell, 'The Sceptical Electorate' in R. Jowell, *British Social Attitudes*, the twelfth Report, Dartmouth, 1995.
13. K. Newton, 'Disillusionment with Democracy', Council of Europe seminar, 8 July 1993.
14. J. Lively and A. Lively (eds), *Democracy in Britain: a Reader* (Blackwell, 1994).

Chapter 7

1. Electoral Commission, *Election 2001: the Official Results* (Politico's, 2001).
2. P. Pulzer, *Political Representation and Elections in Britain* (George Allen and Unwin, 1967).
3. T. Travers, quoted on LGCNet, 8 June 2001.
4. A. Marr, 'Please Vote for Me? But only if you can be bothered. Oh well, never mind', *The Observer*, 9 May 1999.
5. A. Geddes and J Tonge, *Labour's Second Landslide* (Manchester University Press, 2001).
6. G. Evans, 'Political Culture and Voting Participation' in P. Dunleavy et al. (eds), *Developments in British Politics 7* (Palgrave, 2003).
7. D. Clark, 'Placebo Politics', *The Guardian*, 3 June 2004.
8. G. Hoon, op. cit.
9. I. Crewe, T. Fox and J. Alt, *Non-voting in British General Elections 1966–Oct 1974* (University of Lancaster, 1974).
10. R. Putnam, *Bowling Alone* (Simon and Schuster, 2001).
11. F. Devine, *A Qualitative Study of Democracy and Participation in Britain* (ESRC, 2003).

Index

Bold indicates that the term is defined